Realtor Secrets

Get the best from your-

- Real Estate Agent

And save yourself $$$ Thousands!!

By

Paul Gillel

Copyright Notice

Legal disclaimer

The contents of this publication are solely expressed as the opinion of the Author and are the result of the Author's personal experiences as a Salesperson, Sales Manager, Sales Trainer, Auctioneer and Licensee in the Real Estate Industry.

The Author accepts no liability as to the contents of the publication. Further, the Author will accept no liability for any actions taken or losses incurred as a result of the contents of this book being used by any person.

All readers should seek separate professional and appropriate advice before acting upon the suggestions raised in the subject matter of this publication.

Enjoy this book and I hope after reading the contents you can go out and buy or sell your home with more confidence and make more profit for your self

Best wishes

PG

Index of contents

Chapter

Introduction

1. Your Salesperson. What makes a salesperson tick

- The difference between an Agent and a Salesperson.
- Working 24/7.
- How to become a Real Estate Salesperson.
- What to expect from the salesperson as a vendor.
- What to expect from the salesperson as a Buyer.

2. So you want to sell your home.

- How do you want the sale to proceed?
- What if the Salesperson doesn't want your property?
- Are you ready to interview for Salespeople?

3. Let's talk about marketing

- Exclusive marketing.
- Auction Marketing.
- Tender Marketing.
- Grading the Salesperson.

4. Look at the market and setting the price

- The Buyer pool.
- Contributing to the Advertising budget.
- What happens once you've signed the Agency form.
- Buyer mentality.
- What happens at the Open Home.

5. You have a keen Buyer.

- Price is only one part of the offer.
- Discussing the offer from the buyer.
- Counter offering.
- Dates mean Dollars.
- Deposit.
- Contract details and fish hooks.

6. What can a salesperson expect from a buyer?

- Qualifying the buyer.
- A, B and C Buyers..
- Be prepared, as a buyer- Needs versus wants.
- Let the salesperson help you.

7. The Salesperson seems "Pushy"

- The ABC of selling.
- You can't find a house you like.
- Your buying habits and buyer reluctance.
- We already know you like the home.
- Big decisions and little decisions.

8. Basic sales psychology.

- The buying mindset.
- A word of caution.
- More tricks of the trade, the selling trade.

9. You have found the home to buy.

- Contract considerations.
- Make the most of your offer.

10. How good is your Salesperson?

- Advertising.
- Out of town referrals.
- The average Salesperson earns how much!
- The Author gets on his soap box.

11. Assess the level of your competition.

- It's worth doing this calculation.
- I'll hold out for my price.
- I've spent so much on this place.

12. Get down to Negotiating.

- Perception is reality.
- The least desire has the strongest hand.
- Nice guys don't finish first.
- Negotiating tricks.
- Helpful phrases.
- Negotiating lines and their counters.
- Negotiating techniques.

15. . Frequently asked questions.

- Dodgy bids at Auctions.
- Market review meetings.
- Buyer feedback.
- Open homes.
- Mortgagee Auctions.
- Talk to your Solicitor.
- Can I cancel the Agency.
- Complaining about the Agent.
- Changing Agency.
- Referral Network.
- Finance.

17. Final thoughts.

Introduction

Let me introduce myself. I have been involved in the Real Estate industry, direct,for over twelve years. That involvement includes five years as a Salesperson and seven years as a Sales Manager, Owner-operator, trainer, and Auctioneer. I have seldom been motivated by money itself. It seems I have been challenging myself with goals for most of my working life. The nicest part of the goals and challenges I have taken on is that, for the most part, when I have achieved my goals and challenges, I have also made reasonable money as a by product of my efforts.

The next goal I have set myself is to write this book. This one, obviously! It is the book you hold in your hand now and is about Real Estate and how to get the best from your Real Estate Salesperson/ Realtor. Drawing on my Real Estate experience I realise that the industry has a reputation somewhere between Car salesmen and Politicians. 'A necessary nuisance' would sum up most people's attitudes. What I have also realised is that their reputation is not always justified. I would go one step further and say that the reputation is not justified. There are any numbers of Real Estate professionals who are in the industry for the long haul and have made huge efforts to be the best they can be at their chosen career. Unfortunately, there are also a small number of operators who are not so career-minded or as driven in their pursuit of excellence. That minority gives the Media good copy on a slow news day and the poor reputation is perpetuated. My aim in this book, among other things, is to show you how to recognise the good from the bad and also how to get the most value from your dealings with the Real Estate Salespeople.

I love the Real Estate industry!

Why?
Firstly, because it is so easy to excel! As we go through the book you will see why.
Secondly, it's a job where you spend time helping people with problems and often building up long term relationships.

Before we go further, let me explain how the book is set up and the reasoning behind that set up.
For the first section, I will be looking at what you can reasonably expect in your relationship with your Salesperson and also what he can reasonably expect from you. We'll take a look at why I believe you are better off using a Real Estate salesperson to market your home. Secondly we'll take a look at typical transactions that occur in selling a home. Thirdly we look at buying a home. Lastly we look at some tips and tricks in negotiating etc that should make or save you a few dollars.

To finish off the introduction, let's talk about why, I believe, you should be using Real Estate salesperson acting under the rules of the Licensed realtor.

What are your options if you don't use a Real Estate salesperson?

- Sell your home yourself without using any agent at all.
- Sell your home through real estate type broker or investor.

What a bold idea, to sell the home yourself. Everyone should try and sell their home themselves first! Then at least they may have some idea of some of the difficulties the Agent has to put up with, every day! Seven days a week!

From a personal point of view, I have twelve years experience of selling homes. Hey, I even trained people how to be Real Estate Salespeople. And if I were looking to sell my home, I'd definitely use a Real Estate Agent!

That's not what you wanted to hear, is it!

Since I have been involved in Real Estate sales and management, I have sold 8 of my own homes or rental Investment properties and purchased 8 properties. Each time, I used an Agency. There are numerous reasons but I'll only mention a few of them.

Firstly and, for me the most important, is the sheer stress of trying to sell my own home. I found that having to write and organise the advertisements, book in the open home times, man the open homes and do all the follow up was a major stress factor. And don't forget that I did all this as my day job! As people come through your home and criticise your décor, area, even your family photos on the wall, it becomes, very quickly, a depressing way of passing your weekend leisure time. Believe me, people do criticise your home and it's not because they are interested in buying, there are people who get their jollies by going to open homes and annoying Real Estate Agents.

Don't think of selling your own home as a way to save yourself money. The people who buy from private sellers automatically expect to negotiate off your price the amount an agent would charge in fees. If you think you will just raise your price to allow for knocking off the agents fees, read the part of this book that explains about pricing your home.

If you don't know how to go about selling your own home, there have been a number of businesses that have started up, with a fanfare of advertising, offering all the equipment, signage and know how to help you sell your own home at a cost far less than the cost of using a Real Estate Agent. Almost without exception, they have shut their doors within six to twelve months! In fact, I am not aware of any business still operating under the above scheme although there could be the odd small one still keeping its head above water. I just haven't heard of it. Does that tell you how effective they were?

The last and most important reason for not trying to sell your own home is this.

The type of people who will sell through "For sale by Owner" deals. In the mind of the buyer, they immediately seem to conjure up a mental image of there being "something not quite right" about the house. Before you blow your top at the last statement, let's look at the buyer/ seller mindset when they think about buying a home. Let's not even focus on buying a home. Let's look at something fairly easy to understand, like buying a TV.

When you buy a TV, it is a reasonably infrequent purchase. You may buy one every five years or so. When the time comes to buy the TV. Firstly you make the decision to buy the TV. Then comes the next decision, from where, or from whom, who do you buy the TV. You aren't an expert on The TV because of the latest technology changes and buying trends. You remember the situation when video recorders first came on the market all those years ago and you had to decide between buying a VHS or a Beta recorder. You consider whether or not to buy your TV from a garage sale or a small advert in the paper from a private seller. Your thought processes usually go along these lines. It should be quite a bit cheaper, shouldn't it? You have a concern about buying from the private TV seller. You don't know him from Adam. He probably won't give you any guarantee. If the TV breaks down after a month or two, you don't know that the seller will fix it under any guarantee that you did manage to get, so you may have to get a solicitor to get the problems fixed. Even if he gives you a guarantee, will he still be around to honour the guarantee? Here's an important one, how will you know if the price he is asking is fair? Why is the guy selling the TV in the first place? What is wrong with it?

Your main concern, in a nutshell, is your own lack of expertise in buying a TV. If something goes wrong, you want to be able, to use the vernacular, to "Sue Someone and get your money back, if it all turns to custard!" Now read the last paragraph again and substitute the word 'House' where the word 'TV' appears.

Did it make sense with the 'house' in there? If all else fails, you can sue the Agent or something along those lines. That is why, by far the vast majority of people buy their infrequent purchases from recognised outlets. It's a peace of mind thing that helps you feel some security when you are not familiar with the product. Now the people that would buy from the private seller are willing to take the gamble. They are usually gamblers by nature who expect a cheaper deal as a compensation for the lack of security or guarantee. The private sellers and the private buyers are great people to deal with because you can haggle over the price. That is, of course if you are a great haggler and a decent gambler. Most of us aren't in that category which is why less than half a percent of all home sales are done privately. So if you are prepared to appeal to only one buyer in every two hundred potential customers for your home, then maybe you should consider selling privately. And be prepared to wait on the market for a very long time until the right gambler comes along to lock wits with you. As a final thought on the subject, think of this point. Fully eighty percent of FSBO (Pronounced Fizzbo's- For Sale By Owner) place their property in the hands of Real Estate Agents within 3 months of their trying to sell it themselves. This book is aimed at getting the best from your Real Estate Agent, although the private seller/ buyer will also pick up some excellent advice. Let's move on to talk about the Real Estate salesperson you might meet, and what makes them tick.

Disclaimer and note to Readers:

The comments made in this book offer good and sound advice in a generalised manner. Real Estate sales legislation will vary greatly from Country to Country and the contents of this book are not aimed at covering any one specific set of rules.

The advice offered is generally aimed at how to deal with the salesperson you will be in contact with and react against some of the tactics they may use.

Chapter 1- Your Salesperson

Let's look first at what makes up the average Real Estate Salesperson.

The average earnings for a Salesperson in a financial year would possibly be around $31,000 for the whole year!

Let's look at that figure for a minute or two.

It costs the average Salesperson around $12,000 every year to stay in the industry. His costs include the running and purchase/depreciation of a vehicle, his home phone, his mobile phone, gifts to satisfied clients, and personal promotion costs, above what his Office is funding.

From a different perspective, probably only 30% of all Salespeople in the industry will earn in excess of $100,000 per year. Some of those 30% will earn up to and over $200,000! A select few will earn in excess of a Million dollars! When you factor in those earnings, the average earnings of the other 70% would probably not exceed $22,000 per year. Remember that they still have to pay out around $12,000 to be in the business!

To earn these commissions, they are often working seven days a week and to get a deal together or secure a listing they may still be working at 9.00 p.m. or 10.00 p.m. at night!

Why do the low earners stay in the business?

It beats me!
I used to tell all my team that if they could not earn in excess of $30,000 they should get out of the business and go on the dole. The nett pay is just about as good and the hours are definitely better!
Early in the 1990's Real Estate used to be regarded as an easy option by people who were out of work or wanted a career change. It almost became a dumping ground for people who could not get a job elsewhere!

For myself, I had sold my retail business and actually wanted to "have a go" at Real Estate. I had had an unfortunate experience with a poor Real Estate Salesperson (more on that later) and I also had friends in the industry that told me I would be quite good at assisting people with their housing decisions.

Nowadays, there are relatively few people looking to start in Real Estate and I believe that is a positive step for our industry and a distinct advantage for our clients.

To start in Real Estate as a salesperson, everybody has to sit a basic course of study and pass a test. It is, I consider, a fairly minimal requirement for someone who will be advising you on the best way to market your most valuable asset.

Over the last ten years, the drop out rate for new Salespeople is something like 50% in their first year and a further 30% in the second year. That means that of twenty new Salespeople starting today in Real Estate, there would only be four or perhaps five of the twenty still left in the industry in two years time! As I look around in my location today, there are maybe ten salespeople still in the industry that were working in the industry when I first started in 1989. That is ten people out of the one hundred and ten Salespeople that work in our town in Real Estate today!

Does that give you some indication of how tough the Real Estate industry is?

Think on this point also. Of every ten Salespeople that come to your home probably seven of the ten have less than two years experience at selling Real Estate!

Is that a frightening thought?

 It would be for me as a vendor!

Let me repeat an earlier statement I made.

I love the Real Estate industry!

Why? Because it is so easy to be good at it!

Why is it so easy? Because the average standard and experience of my competition is not that hard to beat.

Later we will go into the most common complaints we hear about Salespeople and you may find some of them familiar.

During the course of this book I will be referring to Salespeople as "He" I don't wish to be sexist, but if I point out now that when I say 'He' I actually mean "He or She", it saves me writing out He/She at least 500 times! In the dictionary, the term 'Man' embraces 'Woman'. I kind of like that and we don't need to go further on that in a Real Estate context!

The difference between an Agent and a Salesperson.

The public mistakenly call Real Estate Salespersons 'Agents'. If I may correct that anomaly here, it would be appropriate.

A Real Estate **Agent**, in my country, is a person who has at least three years experience within the Real Estate profession, has passed a number of exams in such subjects as Real Estate Law, Appraisal, Accountancy, Building, Property Management etc, and has applied to the Real Estate governing body for a licence to open a Real Estate Office. That person becomes the licensee of the office. That **Agent** can then invite people to work under his licence as his **Salespeople**.

The rules are fairly similar in every country. It ensures that the office is led by an experienced person who has agreed to conform to all the rules of the industry for his state or country.

Salespeople can only sell property through an Agent's licence. Salespeople, usually, will also have to apply to the governing body for a Salesperson's ticket which is attached to the Agent's licence. The Salespeople are all self employed and work totally for commission on any sales that eventuate through their efforts. In recent years, the rules have tightened considerably.

Although you may only ever deal with the Salesperson when you sell your home, you are, in point of law, dealing with the Agent or licence holder.

A common commission arrangement for the Salespeople would be that the Agent keeps half of the total fee charged to you. The Salesperson that sells the home will get 25% of the total fee and the Salesperson who first brought the listing into the Agents office will receive the other 25% of the total fee. There will be numerous minor variations of that split but that will be pretty close to an average for maybe 95% of all Real Estate Offices.

What does the Agent do for his 50% of the fee?

An unbelievable amount!

I say that with the confidence of having owned or part owned four Real Estate Offices!
The Agent sets up the Office. That means paying rent /phones /electric/ insurance/ administrative staff/Auditors etc. etc. He is also responsible for training the salesperson If you like, the Agent takes the biggest gamble of all.

The Salesperson may have to take a punt on wearing the cost of perhaps, as we said before, $12,000 to keep "his business" going for the year. The Agent commits to an expenditure in excess of $100,000 per year to keep his doors open. With office lease commitments and, say, the lease of photocopiers, faxes computers etc, the commitment may be for a minimum of $100,000 per year for 5 years! When you first open an Office, it can be pretty nerve wracking stuff.

The Agent then has to attract Salespeople who will want to work under his licence to generate income to start paying his bills. The Agent is then expected to train and motivate and monitor the activities of his new team.

At all times, the Agent is held liable for the actions of his sales team. When you sue a Salesperson for any wrongdoing, it is the Agent who will usually be hauled up in front of the disciplinary bench for failing to control his team. The salesperson may still get the bullet, but the Agent will also be hauled over the coals in most circumstances.

If you started to have some sympathy for the Salesperson a little earlier, now would be a good time to spare a thought for the Agent as well!

Working 24/7

If you are not familiar with the term, working 24/7 means working 24 hours a day for 7 days every week. The Agent /Salesperson does not work 24/7. It just seems that way!

With the advent of the Internet, the Salesperson may get a call at 2.00 a.m. from an enquirer in the USA who has seen the listing on the Agent's website. It doesn't happen often, fortunately, but it does happen!

When I say 24/7, imagine if your customers at your workplace felt entitled to ring you with a query at 6.30 a.m. in the morning or perhaps 10.00 p.m. at night. *Would you be happy?* Probably not. But that is the Salesperson's lot. The company's stock is advertised in the paper and some potential buyer spots an interesting home in the paper and gives you a ring to ask about it. Whether it is midday or late evening you still have to be polite. You also have to be switched on into work mode immediately to try and capture that client's interest. With the advent of mobile phones, you may be out at a social function and have taken your 'mobile' with you and a client rings. The Salesperson, again, has to immediately be in work mode.

Remember always, that if the Salesperson has no clients, he is unemployed and won't eat!

I would say that the average Salesperson is on duty for 7 days a week and probably has to be ready to switch in to work mode for 14 hours a day. So let's call him a 14/7 worker.

Having put in the hard yards as both a Salesperson and as a Licensee/Agent, I know how hard some Agents work and I don't begrudge them a single cent of their earnings provided they work ethically and within the bounds set down by the local industry authority.

How do you become a Real Estate Salesperson?

It is not that hard to 'get into Real Estate'. The basic requirements are that you undertake a study course of instruction, which gives you a theoretical grounding in the basic situations you may come up against while selling Real Estate. The course can be taken by correspondence or by evening classes or by a course held in the classroom. It has been said that the educational level in the course is equivalent to a fifth form classroom level.

On passing the course, the candidate can then apply to work for a Real Estate Office. The Owner of the Real Estate Office than applies to the local industry authority for a Salesperson's ticket for the applicant to be attached to the Owner's operating licence. At that point, the student can go out and start selling homes! Now that is quite a scary thought!

In actuality, because of the responsibility that the Office owner has, there is an obligation to train and monitor the new Salesperson for a period until the Agent is satisfied the new Salesperson has reached a sufficient level of competency.

What that level of competence is, is left to the Agent to decide.

If the new Salesperson commits a *faux pas*, the Authority initially takes the Agent to task for not having sufficient control of his Salesperson. If any Salesperson commits a serious breach, that Salesperson can have his Salesperson's ticket removed by the Real Estate Agents Licensing Board but that happens very rarely.

When a new Salesperson joins an office attached to one of the big franchise brands , it is usual for the Salesperson to be sent on a training course, which can last between 3 days and 2 weeks. This course is more geared to teaching the salesperson some selling skills. This is the real training that sets up a new salesperson to handle the sale of your home.

If a new Salesperson starts with an independent Office, any training is left to the Manager and that can sometimes be very hit and miss.

In the days not long gone by, maybe only two or three years ago in fact, there was in place a "Bums on Seats" mentality towards recruiting new Salespersons. If they passed the initial new Salesperson's course and also could read and write, then they got a job.

The rationale behind that mentality was that 'Bigger is Better'. If my Office had fifteen Salespeople and your Office only had ten Salespeople, then my office was bigger and better in the public's uninformed opinion. It did not matter that all my team were brand new to the industry and your team were all ten year veterans. The public had bought into the 'Bigger is Better' idea and it has stuck around for a long time. To a degree, the public was at fault for pushing that perception back at the Offices. The nett result was that Offices would take on anyone to give the impression they were the biggest Office in town. It got to the stage where, if you read the list of Salespeople closely, in their advert, you came across one person whose job title was 'Director of First Impressions' (the receptionist) or 'Media Relations' (the girl who spent one day a week typing up the open homes for that week's advert). Because the public bought into this hype, along with the 'Bums on Seats' policy other Offices had to go along with it and it soon became the norm for all Offices.

Nowadays, sanity prevails and Offices are investing more time and effort and money into training new recruits. The upside of this is that fewer new Salespeople are being taken on and the average quality of the Salesperson is rising.

A word here for the industry authorities. They actively promote the up skilling of all Salespeople in order for the Industry image, as a whole, to lift itself. They usually run a series of talks through the year to bring a Salesperson up to date with current topics and legislation. This can form part of the twelve hours training each salesperson has to undertake.

What can you expect from your Agent or Salesperson?

- Honesty
- Professional attitudes and standards
- Integrity
- Marketing expertise in promoting your property.
- Awareness of local factors in determining fair market values.
- Familiarity with the technology.
- Any number of other factors that will ensure they are working in your best interests.

The reality is, unfortunately, that the way our industry is set up, being totally performance and commission based, you cannot guarantee all of the above.

> *If the Salesperson has not made a sale for three months, can you guarantee his neutrality when it comes to negotiating on your behalf?*

If the Salesperson has only been in the industry for three months, how can he have a sound knowledge base on which to accurately assess your homes true market value?

The sad fact is, that if I were seeking to sell my home I would first ask my friends and associates to recommend a Salesperson or agency to me. I would then ask that Salesperson if he would mind my approaching some of his previous clients for their opinion of his performance. If you were hiring someone at your work, wouldn't you ask for references?

What can you expect from your Agent or Salesperson?

As a vendor.

All of the above mentioned qualities are vital to you in getting the best price for your home. It is your most valuable asset.

One thing most vendors don't fully realise when they sell a home is that they still owe money to the bank.

Follow me with this please. No matter what you sell your home for, you still owe the same amount to the bank. So when you drop your price in the marketing, or when you drop your price in the negotiating stage, any price drop comes out of <u>your share of the proceeds</u>!

How easy is it to listen to the Salesperson when they suggest a price drop and not remember that it is you who are tossing maybe $5,000 away without blinking!

As a Homeowner, I would be expecting that the Salesperson would be totally on my side and not trying to make the sale easier for himself so he could eat!

As a buyer.

A word of caution here for buyers. If you are working with a Salesperson who is taking you to see properties that are above your price range but is telling you that the owners will take an amount in your price range, remember his exact words. If he states to you that the owners will take, say, $150,000, and you make an offer based on his assertion, you can have a reasonable expectation of making a successful purchase at that price! If he comes back and says you will have to pay $155,000 you have a very good case for paying only $150,000 and making the Salesperson or the Agent come up with the balance! It is all to do with your rights as a consumer and salespeople are encouraged to not mislead the buyers with false hopes of possible price expectations

That is a tough call to make for me as an Agent/ Author but it has happened in our Office and we were obliged to reduce our fees by $3,000 to make the deal happen. The alternative was to lose the seller and the buyer and to face a possible hearing in the Consumer Affairs Tribunal with a potential fine of $20,000 plus costs for making misleading statements. The Salesperson was totally out of order but was only carrying on a practise that is sadly becoming more widespread. He sought employment with another office, very shortly after this event occurred!

What your 'Agent' should be able to expect from you?

Honesty and openness.

It is often hard to be honest and open with someone you have only just met. You are not going to share your financial problems with him or you are not going to tell him that you are splitting up with your partner and that is the reason for the sale.

Here's a wee secret for you to think about.

The better Salespeople are often able to read between the lines of what you are saying and they can usually tell very quickly when there is a problem behind the sale. Unfortunately, it is not easy for them to say that they know, as many people are a little embarrassed to be that open with a relative stranger. I used to ask the vendor at the conclusion of the listing interview to tell me what their motivation for selling was. Then I would shut up and let them tell me.

If I "knew" there was a problem and the vendor would not relate it, I knew that I had a problem as well.

The Salesperson has to build a relationship of trust first with the vendor (or the buyer) and that time of trust-building and acceptance can vary greatly from client to client. Once the vendor has opened up to the Salesperson, it is often a lot less stressful for the client as they are now happy with the Salesperson they have employed, and the sale eventuates quicker with all parties working together.

As I have stated earlier, before you select a Salesperson to market your home, ask around at work or in the neighbourhood for the name of a Salesperson that one of your colleagues has used and is willing to recommend, or, even better, a Salesperson that they can warn you against using!

When your friend or colleague recommends a salesperson or a Real Estate office, ask them why they recommend them.

- Prompt service
- Good communications
- Great service
- Lots of open homes
- Aggressive
- honesty
- Non aggressive

It may be that the qualities that appealed to your colleague are not the qualities you are looking for if your degree of motivation is different than that of your friend.

If you take nothing else from this chapter, remember this:

Always ask your friends and colleagues to recommend a salesperson that they were happy dealing with.

Chapter 2 - So you want to sell your home?

Before you get on the phone to ring the two or three Salespeople that your friends have recommended, do some homework first. Prepare yourself for interviewing these Salespeople. Make sure you know what is important *to you* before you hire a Salesperson.

Do you want?

- A speedy sale
- Top price
- High profile marketing
- Weekly open homes
- A sign on your front lawn
- An Internet presence
- To be sold by a certain date
- Weekly written reports from your salesperson
- A high pressure Salesperson
- An Auction marketing programme
- An exclusive marketing programme
- A general or multilist marketing programme
- A Salesperson that has few other listings
- A very active Salesperson that has loads of other stock to market as well as your own home

All well-trained and top-earning Salespeople will treat the listing interview as a job interview and should come well prepared. They should have with them a listing kit that shows you the advantages of the various marketing programmes, the advantages (to you!) of contributing to the advertising profile, some of their previous successes etc, industry qualifications and awards etc.

If you can determine before this job interview what you want out of the deal you will be better prepared to question the prospective Salesperson on his product line.

Let's run through a few of the points listed above and see how they affect you.

- **A speedy sale**.

    There is an average length of time for all sales to occur. Let's say it is 60 days in your location. Another assumption. Your home is worth approx $200,000. If you want a speedy sale, the chances are you will have to drop your expectations on price. If you wanted to sell your home in one day you may have to drop your price to, say, $160,000 and all the Salespeople in the Office will be frantically herding their buyers through your home, as it is a bargain. If you wanted $250,000 for the property you may have to wait for a couple of years or more to sell, until the market values around you reach the higher price you want. You would get very little activity from the Salespeople in the Office, as they could not reasonably be expected to waste their time and effort on taking buyers to a home that is patently overpriced, unless they are using your home and its inflated price to make another home on the books look better value in comparison to your home. If you want the $200,000, you can reasonably anticipate a sale within the 60-day mark. Later on we will look at factors that affect your house prices and can change your value within days without you realising it.

- **<u>Top Price</u>**. You can get top price if you are prepared to wait. And wait, and wait! Unless your home has that certain something that excites the buyer, he is comparing it to all the other homes he has seen. If you were buying a car, you would look around a few caryards and compare prices, wouldn't you? You are looking for, say a 2012 Cadillac and after looking at 3 or 4 yards you pick out one car at one yard as your preferred choice. You may say to the car salesperson that you will buy that car for X dollars or you will go to the other yard where you can get the same car for $1,000 less. That would be smart business wouldn't it? The same thing happens with house buyers. Your Salesperson is familiar with all the houses in your price range that he has on his books. Here's another thing to think about. The buyers have seen possibly five times that number of houses on today's market by viewing homes with other agencies and are quite probably better informed on all the available homes in your price range than you or your Salesperson! They won't pay over the odds for your home. Just as you comparison shopped for the 2012 Cadillac and became better informed on values, the buyers for your home also comparison shopped and know if your asking price is over the top. So, if you want a price that is over the top, be prepared to wait for a very long time!

- **High profile marketing**.

It's a great idea! In the Main paper in a Saturday issue, there are over 25,000 homes advertised for sale. How do you get your home to stand out? You put in a larger advert! Advertising works well. Here is the downside. If you want the larger advert, you have to pay for it! Costs vary greatly around the country. In the Real Estate industry, it is an accepted generalisation that vendors should contribute approximately 1% of the home's value towards their advertising profile. If your home is worth $200,000 then an appropriate ad campaign could reasonably see you digging into your pocket for maybe $2,000. In a major city, advertising costs for the big-ticket homes can go higher than $25,000. In other smaller towns, a high profile ad campaign based around an auction programme will probably fall in the $400 to $800 price range. Don't be tempted to just accept the ad package and price you are offered. Most offices can tailor an Advert campaign to your budget

- **Weekly open homes.**

Ask yourself the question. How quickly do you want to sell? How saleable is your home at the current asking price? Do you prefer to get the sale over with quickly or are you only prepared to sell when you get an offer that is acceptable to you? If you are keen to sell and don't mind the weekly inconvenience of open homes etc, my suggestion would be to have an open home every week. Put down on your list of questions to ask your prospective Salesperson, "How often do you do open homes?" Liken it to going to the dentist and he says you need five fillings and one tooth pulled. Do you get the pain over and done within one session or do you make six separate appointments? All the pain and inconvenience in one brief period or do you spread it out over a longer period and take a lower pain level? It's your call.

- **A sign on your front lawn.** This is one of the most frequently raised objections I hear at a listing presentation. Do I need to have a sign on my lawn? There probably is a long answer but it is just a longer version of the short answer, which is"Definitely YES!" I suppose the long answer would be along the lines of "Definitely YES and make it as big as possible!" That is probably not the answer you wanted but look at it from this point of view. Remember earlier when I said the Salesperson does not work 24/7? Well the sign does! Most buyers will cruise their intended neighbourhood before approaching a Salesperson. If they see a place they like with a sign outside, they will in all likelihood use their mobile phone to ring the Salesperson from outside the house to make their initial enquiry. No sign outside means it is being kept a secret. It's very hard to sell something that is a secret! Don't be too concerned about the neighbours knowing you are on the market. Often an enquiry will come from a neighbour's friend who wants to live near their neighbour! Get the sign up as quickly as you can and make it a big one!

- **An Internet presence**.

  Most Offices have a free internet site for their clients and with some of the multi-national groups (Century 21, Harcourt's, LJ Hookers etc) there is often a steady source of enquiry from overseas

- **To be sold by a certain date.** If you have a target date for moving (you want to be in the new home by April 15 so little Johnny can start at his new school on the first day of the new term), tell the Salesperson as soon as you can and ask for his suggestions. As a guideline, it will usually take an average of a month from the time the sale goes unconditional until the settlement occurs. Add on to that the average time for an offer to go unconditional (two weeks) and add to that the average sale time in your area (60 days), and you should quickly realise that to move in to the new home by April 15 you have to be on the market by January the 1st at the latest. The two options open to you if you want to move quickly, are either a high profile (Auction?) campaign or a drop in your price expectations! Either way, talk to your Salesperson as soon as you can about your time constraint

- **Weekly written reports from your Salesperson.**

You need your Salesperson to keep you up to date with all that is happening with the marketing of your home. Weekly written reports are the minimum standard you should expect. Give the following instruction to your Salesperson. 'I want to hear what **I need** to hear and not what you **think I want** to hear.' If all the buyers going through your home are saying it is overpriced or the garage needs an auto door opener, you really need to hear that feedback. If the Salesperson is telling you week after week that "The market is quiet, we'll try a different time next week for the open home", you are not being kept up to date with the market. Here's a tip. Send in a friend to the open home and tell him to say that the home is 10% over the top in price. Get your friend to tell you the Salesperson's reaction and attitude and also wait for the feedback from your Salesperson in his next weekly report. It could be a real eye opener for you!

- **A high-pressure Salesperson.** Who will he be putting the pressure on? You or the buyer? Can you handle yourself against a high-pressure Salesperson? It's something to think about.

- **An Auction marketing programme.** Personally, I am a keen advocate of Property Auctions provided they are sold correctly to the vendor. By that I mean I am against the usual sales patter of the Salesperson painting a scenario of the auction day happening with a crowd of excited bidders all eagerly thrusting their fingers skyward and paying 20% over the market price in their excitement. It does happen. Occasionally. Very occasionally! The reality is that only 10% of auctions sell under the hammer. Perhaps 60% sell before the auction day and another 20% sell in the two months following the auction. 10% will never sell because the vendor's expectations are just too high or they take the property off the market. So why do I recommend auctions? The concept of auction marketing should, I believe, be sold as a way of marketing within a time frame that puts pressure on the buyers to perform (arrange finance etc) on or before a certain date. If I may elaborate it will become clearer.

When a prospective buyer views an auction property, without fail, the question soon arises from the potential buyer, "So, what will they take for it?" The wise Salesperson will respond by not giving away their vendor's expectations, but will turn the question back and ask the buyer what do they think it will sell for, on the day. If the buyer says $190,000, my usual response would be to suggest "On the day, it may possibly go for that, if there are no other bidders in the room, or it could go as high as $225,000 if there are a few bidders around showing interest. If you have some interest in the property at $190,000 today, why not make an offer for that amount to the vendors today? Provided you can go unconditional before the Auction day, you may be able to avoid having to pay the premium price of $225,000". If the buyer did submit an offer, I would advise the vendor of all interest received up to that point to be considered in their thoughts on the offer submitted. 60% of auction properties sell prior to the auction day! The concept of auction marketing should be promoted as a very effective means *of putting pressure on a buyer to get their act together*. Often the buyer will be motivated by a fear of loss and that is why so many homes sell prior to the Auction day. It worked very well for me as a Salesperson and it should work well you as a vendor provided your Salesperson is skilled and has the right mindset.

- **An exclusive marketing programme OR A general or Multilist marketing programme.** Opinion may be divided here. As a personal preference I only ever worked for vendors who listed exclusively with my Office or me. If they made a commitment to me by giving me a listing, exclusive to my office, for three months I would commit to them with my allocation of available time and budget.

Here is another secret for you to think about.

In a normal three month marketing period, up to 85% of Auction or Tender listings will sell, 60% of all Exclusive listings will sell, only 3 % of general listings/Multilist will sell. The Offices will often not commit advertising dollars etc. to the general listings. The commission structure mentioned earlier is also amended for general listings. For bringing in an Auction or Exclusive listing the Salesperson gets approx. 25% of the total commission when it sells. For bringing in a general listing, the listing fee drops to 10% of the overall fee. So that is why Salespeople prefer to deal with Exclusive or Auction listings. They have a twenty times better chance of a sale with an exclusive listing than a general and the pay is 2 ½ times better than for selling a general listing. These pay rates may differ from Office to Office but they are applicable to probably 90% of all Offices.

- **Do you employ a Salesperson that has few other listings or a very active Salesperson that has loads of other stock to market as well as your own home?**
Do they have little stock by choice so that they can focus more on each individually or do they have loads of stock so they can cover all price ranges of the market? It really comes down to the personality of the individual Salesperson. At an Office I worked in back in 1992, on one side of me sat Kelly with never more than five listings and on the other side of me sat Rosie who never seemed to have less than twenty-five listings. Kelly was a quiet, intense and focussed lady who seemed to sell 90% of her own listings. Rosie was an outgoing, bubbly lady who just kept putting the sales on the board. I sat in between these two

extremes with my consistent portfolio of between fourteen and eighteen listings. We were all good performers within our office. At the end of the year, Rosie out-earned Kelly by the grand total of $79.55! (I came third, $500 behind Kelly). For myself I would have chosen the Salesperson whose personality I got on better with (Rosie) - all other things being equal.

What if the Salesperson doesn't want *you* as a vendor!

Okay, we've had a look at things from your side. Now let's look at them from the Salesperson's viewpoint.

Why should he want to work for you?

To make some money for *himself* is the reason the Salesperson wants to secure your listing for his office. That would be sufficient reason to want the listing.

Think of this scenario please. If you offer him the listing of your home at a price that is perhaps 20% over what the market will pay should he take your listing? For me the answer is a very simple and solid **No**! If I am a switched on and focussed Salesperson who is spending my own money on personal promotion, and putting in my 14/7 work week, why on earth should I waste my time on something that is not saleable on the market today at a price that a reasonably educated buyer will want to pay?

I have shown the Vendor ample evidence of local values and demonstrated how I reached my estimate of the value of his home. If he is unwilling to meet the market and list it within 5% or 10% of Fair Market Value (FMV) I should explain to the vendor that I or my Office would be unable to meet his price expectations and rather than string him along for three months chipping away at his price, I would be doing him a greater favour by suggesting he take his listing to another Company. Then I make a diary note to contact him again in three months to check his motivation and price.

That was how I handled an overpriced listing. A Salesperson that is struggling to get or keep listings will take in any listing at any price. That is the sign of a poor Salesperson who is very unlikely to sell your home for you!

If a Salesperson estimates the value of your home at $200,000 and you want it listed at $230.000, there is virtually no chance of him making any money from your listing. That should be self-evident? So what kind of Salesperson would agree to take on that listing? Unfortunately, only a poor or weak Salesperson. As an estimate, I figured on every listing taking approx two hours per week of my time over a four-week period. Some weeks I may have spent eight hours on one listing and then nothing, beyond weekly reports, for the next three weeks. An average of two hours per listing per week would be a reasonable time allocation.

Why anyone would commit to taking on an overpriced listing that will commit them to probably twenty-six or thirty hours of work, expense and skill for three months with an almost zero expectation of any reward, eludes me. Fortunately, the type of Salesperson that will take that type of listing will only keep it warm for the three months so it is relatively easy to come along after the three months and pick it up at the correct market price.

When is it acceptable for a Salesperson to decline a listing?

Any time he or she wants to decline it!

As a matter of fact, from my experience, if a Salesperson had the nerve to decline a listing, it would probably raise that Salesperson in my estimation. It can mean one, or both, of two things. He knows he will be wasting his time working on the listing (it is overpriced or the vendor is unreasonable in his expectations) or he has enough personal stock of good quality that he would not be able to fully service your listing without dropping better quality stock of his own. Either way, you have a good Salesperson who can probably do the job well and he has a vendor with unreasonable price expectations (that means you, by the way).

My favourite type of vendor was always the one who tried to take control of the situation at the listing interview. They would tell me what they wanted me to do, how much they wanted the home listed at, what was the minimum they would take, how many open homes etc. etc.

Then I would explain that, from my viewpoint, I was the expert in marketing property and I would be using all my skills to achieve the best price that a buyer would pay them, for their home, in the current market. That is what they would be employing me for, and, because of the way I conduct my business, a friend had recommended me to them. If they wanted to be the experts ahead of my expertise they should work with a Salesperson who wanted or needed guidance. So what was it to be? We would work as a team together and sell the home or would they prefer to call all the shots in which case I would have to withdraw?

I did not turn down many listings. But to get on my books, there had to be a better than even chance I would make some reward for my efforts. If you think about it, would you expect any other professional or trades person to take on a job where they knew they would lose money on the job?

By the way, if ever you feel aggrieved that a Salesperson will not take on your listing you are quite entitled to get the Salesperson's boss on the phone and complain. At the very least, the boss will usually check his Salesperson's appraisal of your home and confirm or decry the Salesperson's valuing skills.

Are you ready to interview the Salesperson?

Okay, so you have had the Salesperson round to look at your home and he is coming back later with sales information to give you an idea of your home's value and to propose a marketing plan.

Now you should readying yourself for the interview. Preparing yourself for the questions you want to ask of your future employee. Does this all sound a little scary? Interviews, employees, marketing proposals etc. What if you had $200,000 in the bank and you decided to invest it? Would you walk down the road until you saw the first investment broker and write him a cheque? Or would you do a little homework first? Get some questions you wanted answering? Ask your friends if they could recommend a broker that they had been satisfied with? What is the difference between $200,000 in the bank and $200,000 in bricks and mortar? Think about it!

I'm going to take things a little out of order here. In this chapter I want you to think about where you are coming from with your wish to sell your home. We have already asked ourselves a number of questions about what we want from the sale. Such questions as: a speedy sale, top price etc have been covered already. Now let's look at your home and your perception of its value and marketability. In the next chapter we'll give you a few ideas on how to grade your prospective salesperson.

You already have some idea of your home's value, don't you? Well the one down the road sold for $215,000 last December and their place had a smaller garden than yours, so yours must be worth probably another $10,000 on top of that. It would be nice to think that, but there are so many factors to consider here.

Firstly, *did* the one down the road sell for $215,000 or is that the figure the owner fed to you? The Salesperson should have the accurate sale figure from Valuation NZ to make an accurate comparison.

Secondly, who says that buyers today want larger grounds? There is a growing trend towards smaller and easier care sections. This has been brought about by the changing social set up in New . With more businesses open at the weekend, families are finding it hard to maintain large sections comfortably and the good old fashioned "quarter acre" is a thing of the past, along with vinyl records! The larger section may actually reduce the home's appeal and price!

There are a number of factors for the Salesperson to consider when estimating the likely sale price of a home. Location is always high on the list; size of home and its amenities; garden style (easy care) is another factor along with the garaging etc. Often we cannot compare apples with apples. In the middle to upper price ranges, we, as appraisers, have to juggle things like 'is a double garage with auto door as appealing to a buyer as maybe a 4th bedroom?'
As Salespeople we see our role in appraising homes as trying to interpret what we feel we can encourage a buyer to pay for the home. Let's take that part again as it is probably one of the more important things you should take away from reading this book

> *As Salespeople we see our role in appraising homes as trying to interpret what we feel we can encourage a buyer to pay for the home.*

We do not see ourselves as valuers coming up with a definitive quote of the home's value. There is quite a difference in those two mindsets. If it is not apparent to you at first, think about it until you can understand where we are coming from.

The biggest single factors in appraising your home are the state of the market and the amount of competition in your price range. These factors are also the factors that fluctuate most quickly.

This may get a little complicated so bear with me please.

How does the number of homes on the market affect the value on my home?

Go back in to your memory banks please. Did you ever own a home in a first home subdivision? Remember them? A street with maybe one hundred new homes - Fibro-plank exterior, iron roof, aluminium joinery, Housing Corp loans? All pretty much the same type of size and construction quality.

If you did not own one like the example, use your imagination please. This is quite a fundamental concept for you to grasp.

Ten years after they were built, the people started to move from these homes up into the second home level and the homes in the street started to come onto the market. As you walked down that street the *average* home was worth, say $60,000, and the average home by then had a single garage and a sealed driveway. If it had a double garage, it was worth maybe $62,500. If it was without any garage it was only worth $57,000. You get the picture? All the homes were nearly identical and pricing was easy to figure out.

In the street of one hundred homes, fifteen of the homes all come on the market within a very short time frame and all within a price range of $59,000 to $63,000. The market is good and people are looking to move into the street. It has become a desirable area for the price range. Sales are averaging around $61,000 and ten of the homes sell. The situation arises where there are more buyers than homes so the price goes up a little. Two of the homes sell for $63,000. Only three more to sell. Great stuff! The asking price on these homes has shot up to $67,500 and another one sells for $66,000.

The law of supply and demand has kicked in. The shortage of homes to buy has allowed the prices to rise by 10% in a very short time.

Seeing the great prices these homes are getting, another ten of the neighbours place their homes on the market to make a killing. Unfortunately, the extra homes mean that the buyers can be a little more leisurely in their purchase. Maybe they can play off one owner against the other, in the same manner you did when you were buying your 2012 Cadillac (remember?). What happens next is fairly predictable. With the oversupply of homes, prices drop quickly and within a month or two the average sale price is now down to $59,500.

Equate that easy illustration to the location in which you live. Don't look at it as just one street. Look at the situation, at the amount of competition in your price range. How many other homes are there on the market today within five kilometres of your home and within 8% of your hoped for price range? Ask the Salesperson how many sales in your price range have been made in the last three months. Ask him if he can guesstimate how many homes in your price range and area are on the market. Divide the one answer by the other.

Fifteen sales per month and forty-five homes as market/price competition means that the market has three months supply of homes, which is pretty good. You stand a reasonable chance of a sale within three months, if all other factors are equal. Fifteen sales and one hundred and fifty homes on the market means, on average, you could be waiting ten months for a sale! That is bad news. Now you may have to consider a high profile ad campaign to lift the profile of your home above the others. Alternatively, you may consider a price drop to make your home seem like greater value. If you consider the analogy of a simple tin of baked beans, you may find it easier to grasp the concept. Watties Beans are dearer than the competition, but Watties have brand name acceptance of quality merchandise. An unknown brand cannot compete on brand quality so has to compete for a buyer by being cheaper in price. The more tins of beans there are on the shelf, the more cutthroat the pricing has to be! It's called the supply demand ratio and it certainly applies to the housing market!

The role of the Salesperson at the listing interview is to interpret how your home will sit against its competition. Quite often, the sale that happened six months ago is irrelevant to today's market. That perception of your home's value will change if another ten homes in your price range come on the market that same week because the supply / demand equation has been altered. If the 6.00 p.m. news tonight leads with a story that tells us of an increase in finance interest rates of 3% happening in seven days, that would probably also have a major impact on your house value as buyer confidence fluctuates.

A small town or a large suburb in a major town is a relatively small economy and consequently is so very interdependent on most of the other parts of the economy.

Here is a supposition for you to think about. The government removes the need for state house tenants to pay market rents. Does that have an impact on the value of your $200,000 home?
Sorry to say, the answer is yes!

How??
Work with me on this one please.

State house/welfare homes/assisted housing tenants get cheap rents.
Tenants in private rental accommodation want to get cheap rent as well.
Private landlords have to reduce their rental rates to keep their tenants or they will move out and the Landlord will have no income. Because of the lower return on their rental investments, the value of the rental properties decreases (obviously). What was a rental home worth $80,000 has now been reduced to $65,000 or $70,000.

The person who wants to sell his $80,000 first home to move up a notch has to reduce his home selling price to $70,000 or it won't sell. And there is now a glut on the market of rental properties and they are all in the $65,000 to $80,000 range so we have an oversupply, which as we have been shown, means a drop in values or an extended time on the market

When our first home vendor sells his home for (be generous) $68,000 he is now a further $10,000 short of his purchase price for the $110,000 home he wanted to buy. So, the vendor of the $110,000 home drops his price by $10,000 or he will be unable to sell it. These $10,000 price drops carry on right up the chain to your $200,000 home.

Thought you were sitting pretty did you?

I hope you are getting an idea of the difficulty the Salesperson has in estimating a sale price for your home. With so many variables to consider the price estimate could change almost weekly. That is why the smart Salesperson will generally give you a price range. Instead of stating that the home is worth $197,500. He should be saying something along the lines of " I feel your home should have some appeal to a qualified buyer looking to purchase in the range of $192,000 to $200,000."That gives a spread of 4%, which I feel is a little tight. I would usually be looking for a range of 5% to 8% when the market is as unpredictable as it is today.

Right, having gone through all the above, we now get down to the first tactic used by those Salespeople who are not at the "top of their Game". That is my polite way of saying *Inefficient, not overly competent, not overly skilled etc* (I'm sure you understand).

The first and one of the worst tricks is called:-

Buying the listing

You may have called three or four or even five different companies in to appraise your home. Why not? It is a free service they offer isn't it?

They all come back to you with their idea of the price you should make in a sale. The price anticipations are: (along with your thoughts)

- $192,000. - a little low you think.
- $198,000 - "Well we really wanted $200,000"
- $192,000 to 199,000 – "Well 199,000 is pretty close" (don't ignore the 192,000 part)
- $198,000 to $208,000 – "We won't take less than 200,000 after your fees are taken out!"
- $205,000 to $220,000 – "That's more like it!"

So which one do you go for? Did your thought process change with each price offered? We are assuming a Fair Market Value on your home of $200,000. Examine the supporting sales data closely. How many of them used the same properties for comparison and still came up with a different price expectation?

Firstly take a look at the highest price offered. It is way above the others and should probably be ignored. If the other four Salespeople viewed your home and then went away to examine the statistics and did not come up over the $200,000 mark, it would appear that the last Salesperson is trying to 'buy' the listing and buying the listing works like this.

The Salesperson is hoping to get you to sign exclusively with his company for a three month period or longer. He will also try to get some dollars out of you for a contribution to the advertising. Within two weeks of his marketing commencing, he will be back to see you asking you to drop your price as the 'market has turned downwards and the buyers don't see the value at over $200,000!' You have wasted two weeks of marketing and you have committed your home and your advert dollars to this turkey for the next three months. You feel a little angry at having to drop your price so quickly and you feel just a little ripped off.

How to overcome this type of trick? It is not easy really. Ask him to justify his price, given that he is so much higher than the others. If he stutters and stumbles, it is pretty certain he has come up with a price that he thinks you wanted to hear rather than being a little more honest or professional. These Salespeople who buy listings are doing nobody any favours, especially vendors! And should be brought to heel by the vendors!

"Can he, *personally*, guarantee you will get 'in excess of $200,000' for your home or he will put up the shortfall?" is one question that will make him splutter.
After three months and when your home is on the market at its correct price, you may change companies when the agency has finished.

Of the prices quoted above, and all other things being equal, I would probably try the Salesperson that quoted '$198,000 to $208,000' as being near the mark. The lowest one I would dismiss as being too pessimistic. The remaining three are all reasonable close so I may as well go with someone who is optimistic about my property in preference to the pessimistic ones. As I said before, this choice is dependent on *all other factors being equal.*

The next thing to decide is the marketing of your home and whether to advertise a price, a price range or have no price identified in the adverts.

Remember these points:

- *Decide what is important to you in the sale and find a Salesperson who will deliver.*
- *You need to have a good feel about your salesperson. Often it comes down to a gut feeling about him or her.*
- *Don't let any Salesperson feed your ego by 'Buying the listing'*

Chapter 3-Let's talk about the marketing.

To my mind, there are 3 preferred options.

1. Exclusive marketing,
2. Marketing by auction
3. Marketing by tender.

In terms of success rates, Auction marketing beats Exclusive marketing and both are streets ahead of Tender marketing programmes.

My experience in general agency marketing is that it is a waste of your time as well as the Salesperson's and doesn't have a significant success rate, even if you are motivated to meet the market.

Exclusive marketing

Means that you give the marketing of your home exclusively to one Agency for a set time. Usually three months would be the minimum and six months the maximum. That Agency takes on responsibilities to you, as their customer, to be proactive and diligent in the marketing of your home. Signage, open homes, preparation of flyers and brochures, a window card in their office display, internet presence and a small amount of

newspaper advertising would usually be provided free of charge to all exclusive listings. Any extra advertising or larger signage would be available if you funded it as the vendor. The property owner in 99.9% of cases has funded all the large ads and glossy oversize signage for any property you see. Very occasionally the Salesperson will pay for some of the extra advertising, as he may want to get a home sold to make several other deals work. This is definitely the exception to the rule. **Remember this rule,**
#You can have as much profile as you want, if you want to pay for it!

Auction Marketing

We mentioned it before. Auctions are excellent tools if used correctly by an experienced Salesperson. Visit the open homes of other Auction properties and ask the Salesperson "What do they want for this one?" If the Salesperson gives you a price, you may be well advised to steer clear of that Salesperson when selling your own home. The old chestnut of 'lots of buyers paying over the odds in their enthusiasm' is the exception rather than the rule. Unless your home is an exceptional home, you are unlikely to have lots of enthusiastic buyers paying over the odds. If your home is unusual in design and difficult to price accurately, you would be advised to use an auction. If your home is occupying a premium site or has some other feature that people may be willing to pay a premium for, again you should at least consider an auction. When I was selling homes I used auction marketing for probably 50% of my listings, as I was a firm believer in the auction process. My belief in auctions was centred more on my ability to pick out suitable auction vendors rather than auction properties. If the vendor motivation was high and the vendors were ready to meet the market, then I recommended auction marketing. Unfortunately, with many salespeople, it seems today that the prime requirement for auction programmes is the ability of vendors to front up with the advert dollars. Suitability of the property or the vendor sometimes seems of secondary importance.

Tender marketing

Again, it is another way of marketing a property that allows the Salesperson to put pressure on a purchaser to act within a predetermined time frame. Tenders have not yet been widely accepted by ordinary homebuyers so auctions still seem the way to go if you want to have a high impact, short-term promotional campaign on your property. If you are unaware of the tender system, all interested parties are invited to submit their offers to purchase the home in to a sealed envelope. In theory, all the envelopes remained sealed until the time for tenders to close. All offers are then opened at the same time and compared. Often, further negotiations take place with one offeree. With tenders, all offers should be valid for a 7-day period after the tenders close. That allows for negotiations to begin with a second party if the first party's offer is unacceptable.

Ok, that covers the three main types of marketing residential property. Now we want to pick out the best Salesperson who can sell our home.

Think on this scenario for a moment please. You are going in to hospital for surgery. It is a serious level of surgery. You have three surgeons to pick from. One guy has been operating for 35 years, the second for 12 years and the third one only arrived at the hospital last week after graduating three weeks earlier. Which one do you pick?

The new guy would not be my choice. He has the book knowledge but probably lacks experience. The guy with many years of experience may not be the most clued up on the new techniques and that leaves me feeling more comfortable with the other guy who probably has a good experience level and is probably pretty up to date with new innovations etc.

Can you see the parallel to selling your home? I agree the rookie has to get experience somewhere but I don't want him to gain that experience at my (literally) expense. The guy with more experience has been doing it for years. Probably has been doing it the same way for years. In today's fast moving world I want someone who can work with all the modern tools and innovations of today's marketing environment. If that sounds selfish (it probably does!) remember that you pay the same commission for a successful sale irrespective of how competent or incompetent the Salesperson is. Why should you not be getting the best Salesperson in the Office if you are paying the top money for him?

The Salesperson, when he comes to your home, will be trying to convince you that he is the very best Salesperson you can have and that he works for the very best Office in town and that his team are the biggest sales team in town etc. They will all say the same thing to you. If they don't say it, they will probably tell you all the reasons why you should not be dealing with the biggest team etc. Confused?

Remember a few pages back when I suggested you ask yourself some questions about how you wanted to sell your home and what you wanted in a Salesperson? Now is the time you should have the answers to those questions fixed in your mind. While you are talking during the interview.

Grading the Salesperson

Of your Salesperson, here are few things that may crop up or things that you should know the answers to. I have also included a little points scale. The points are totally unscientific in their allocation but if you read the notes below you may get a better feel for the Salesperson.

Experience of the Salesperson. How long has he been involved in selling homes in your area?

> 1 Year or under   = -5 points
> 2-5 years   = 0 points
> More than 5 years = +5 points

The experience of the individual Salesperson is vital. While he may have a vastly experienced team behind him, the actual Salesperson will be representing you at probably 70% of all initial enquiries pertaining to your home sale. You need an experienced Salesperson working as your listing Salesperson.

How many listings does his Office carry as a percentage of the local available market?

> Under 10%   --5 points
> 10-15%   0 points
> 15-20%   +5 points
> Over 20%   +10 points

If his Office has a small market share of listings, his Office will only get a small share of buyer enquiry. That's logical, isn't it? As an experiment, take a drive round your neighbourhood, say within a kilometre. Make a note of all the various Real Estate signs on display and the Salesperson's names on those signs. If your candidate or his company are not figuring highly in that survey, you should ask him why. Maybe they have a strong showing in a lower or higher price range than your home. That is not going to be to your advantage if they don't have a lot of buyer enquiry in your price range or your location.

What is the **company's market share** of sales in the area over the last 6 months?

Under 10%	-5 points
10-15%	0 points
15-20%	+ 5 points
over 20%	+ 10 points

You have heard of the old saying "Success breeds success" haven't you? Trust me it is true! If your prospective Salesperson is part of an unsuccessful team, that is going to impact on your sale in a big way.

How does the Salesperson rank within his own Office?

Consistently in the top 2 or 3 every month for performance   +5 points
Consistently in the top half most months 0 points
Very up and down, finished third 3 months ago etc -5 points

We mentioned earlier that you pay the same rate of commission whether you have a great Salesperson or a dummy. So you may as well have the best.

How do auctions work? Which sales patter does he use?

-5 points --.if he talks of lots of buyers paying over the market.
0 points   --if he talks of using the auction as tool to pressure buyers.
+5 points -- if he says auctions are not suitable for every property.

How open is the Salesperson being with you? If he *automatically* jumps into promoting auctions as the only way to market homes, he may be using your advertising dollars to promote his personal profile irrespective of the suitability of either the property or the vendor for an auction programme.

All of the above questions are questions that the Salesperson will not want to hear. If nothing else, it tells him that he may have an educated vendor on his hands and he will have to be a little careful with any 'puffery' that he may have been tempted to use on you.

Now lets look at his **Presentation or 'listing kit'**

Salesperson 1. He came to view the home and gave you a price on the spot without consulting sales statistics etc. He said you should be thinking of putting in a few dollars towards the ads as the market is pretty quiet and you need to lift your profile. No listing kit shown. Expected to get the listing there and then.

> *Steer clear of this one. If he gave this much effort towards his 'job interview' how much effort will he give when he is actually working for you. – 5 points*

Salesperson 2. Came back for the second visit with an attractively presented folder showing you the price range he thinks your home should sell for. Gave a good explanation of how he reached that conclusion with the recent sales in the area and the current competition you have in the market place. Suggested you sign up exclusively with his company for a three month period. And you could discuss marketing options once you have tested the market for 'a few weeks".

He was doing so well but stopped short of explaining the market forces at work or the probable need for you to contribute to the adverts etc. More intent on getting you hooked in for the three months before he started to work on you. 0 points

Salesperson 3. Did what Salesperson 2 did and then went on further by explaining what the various marketing options available to you were. Explained the need for vendor contributions. Discussed with you the relative merits of marketing with a price, with a price band or without a price. Discussed his perception of his involvement with you and what he would need from you in the marketing (access etc.). Explained that after a period on the market you may have to consider a marketing or price review and tentatively organised a 2 (no more than 3) weekly marketing review-meeting programme with you. At the end of the meeting you felt comfortable that you were dealing with a professional and organised Salesperson that was fully capable of marketing your home and achieving the top result for his client (you)

If you got this good a feeling from this Salesperson you should be working with this guy! + 5 points.

Okay. You have picked your Salesperson. What happens next?

Between you, you fill out the listing form. Answer all the questions fully and honestly. If you have carried out work that needed permits etc did you get the permits? Say you replaced the old Kent fire in the lounge with a new Masport fire. Guess what, it needed a permit! It gets worse! With the Building Act 1992, your local council or authority can no longer give out retrospective permits. That means they cannot just wander round and give a permit after a quick looksee at the job like they used to in the good old days. For a permit to be issued, the inspector has to be satisfied that the job complies completely with the Building Act and it's standards. For the fireplace it means that you will have to pull it out and reinstall it. For the carport round the back of the house, the inspector cannot be certain that the footings were dug deep enough so a permit cannot be issued. For an illegal extension, the inspector has to be certain that the correct insulation was used everywhere so, again, no permit can be issued and you may have a major problem.

When the new prospective purchaser goes down to the council to check out the building files or asks for a builders report, the problem will be revealed. The sale could fall over at that point or you may be forced to drop your price a few thousand dollars to make the sale happen.

Now is the time for you or your Salesperson to go to the local council and examine your building file for any potential problems. In the Current Sale and Purchase agreements used today for selling homes, there is a clause guaranteeing that you applied for consent (permit) for all work carried out, that needed local consent for. You can be held liable for any non-conforming work that you were responsible for. My advice would be for you to get it tidied up on day one of the marketing. Tell your Salesperson what is happening and the time frame for the correction etc.

When you have filled in the form and before the Salesperson asks for your signature, read the small print.

Now read it again.

Did you know that, if you have signed up exclusively with the Salesperson at 4pm today and at 5pm your neighbour offers to buy the home from you, you are still liable to pay the Agent his full commission?

If the Salesperson brings someone along on the last day of the agency but does not make the sale before you cancel his agency, he can maybe still claim his commission from you two months later when the buyer approaches you direct or through another company?

Please read the small print thoroughly. It could save you a lot of pain and a fistful of dollars

Let's take a brief look at the pros and cons of advertising your home with or without a price.

You have 3 options.
- Advertise a set price
- Advertise a price range
- Advertise without a price

Advertise with a set price would be the most common way of selling homes historically. Set the price at, say, $215,000 and let the buyers beat you down to your price of $200,000. Sounds good in theory and has worked well for a long time. The down side is that when you set a price, you often find that you automatically exclude a whole range of buyers on either side of your price. Someone with only $200,000 to spend would probably not look at your price or would not be happy with the Salesperson showing them the home as they are so far away from their spending limit. The buyers looking to spend $220,000 to $240,000 will not want to look below their price range. So, by advertising a set price you are only appealing to a limited number of buyers.

Advertise with a price range. Another good idea with limitations. Say you advertise at $200,000 to $220,000. This should appeal to all buyers from those looking to spend from $190,000 through to, perhaps, those wanting to spend up to $225000. Buyers are happy with the practise, sellers are happy, the Real Estate Offices are happy.

The problem is that the Government is not!

Under the Fair Trading and other consumer protection Acts the Dept of Consumer Affairs takes the view that any price advertised at the lower end of the price range must be the price at which someone can buy the home! They believe that the public has a reasonable right to expect that the bottom price is the lowest price for which they can actually buy the home.

For the Real Estate industry it is difficult to see their logic, as using their logic would mean that if we advertised a home at a set price of $215,000, the public should be regarded as dumb enough to expect that $215,000 is the only price it can be sold for. The logic does not compute and is always in the favour of the buyer.

As always the Real Estate Offices are stuck in the middle of this red tape and the vendors are the ones that lose out. The thing to remember here is that it will take a complaint by a purchaser for anything to happen, so the Real Estate industry continues with price banding and the government keeps warning the industry authority who keeps warning the Real Estate Offices. It's ridiculous and is, I feel, another case of big brother stepping in, in case anybody screams before they are hurt. Generally, if we keep the price bands reasonably tight and advertise them as 'being suitable for the attention of buyers looking to purchase in the price range of ...' there is not a lot of risk of upsetting 'big brother'.

Advertising with no price. My favourite method. Although I prefer to use this style of pricing in conjunction with an auction or tender campaign it can be used with "P.O.A" (Price on application) in the advert.

In theory, with no price mentioned, it should exclude no buyers. In practice we found that it attracted a lot of buyers who were obviously not looking in the price range. Those buyers complained to us about wasting their time so we as an industry started to advertise that bidding was expected from $xxxx. This was to give an indication only of price range.

Again, big brother stepped in. The 'bidding from' price had to be the lowest price that the property could be purchased for and the 'bidding from' price was misleading the poor public again. As an industry, we cannot win. However the 'bidding from' price practice has persisted and unless some buyer complains, the big brother dept have not bothered us again. I guess it is just more examples of the government going overboard with its 'PC' awareness.

Talk to your Salesperson about how you want to handle the price presentation issue. He may have a particular preference that seems to work best in your location

---

Points to remember:
- *Don't ever be afraid to ask the salesperson any question.*
- *If he offers references. Check them.*
- *If he doesn't offer references, ask for them.*
- *Be prepared to contribute to the advertising.*

Chapter 4 - Looking at the market and setting the price

Before you sign on the dotted line, you first have to agree on the price your home will be marketed at. For the sake of this example let's assume you are going to market the home with a set price. You accepted the price range of $198,000 to $208,000 as the suggested selling range but what price do you advertise it at to attract the buyers?

Before we go to that question, let's talk about the "Buyer pool".

The 'Buyer pool'

The 'buyer pool' is the term we use to describe all the people that may want, or be in a position to, buy your home.

On day one of the marketing there may be a hundred potential buyers out there who want to buy a home but have not seen anything they like sufficiently to make an offer to purchase. Some of those buyers have been looking for over five or six months and will not buy until they see exactly what they want or the price is good enough to interest them. Got the picture?

Also in the 'buyer pool' there are perhaps another five to ten new buyers who will join every month. These are buyers who have just sold their home or are moving into the area. The 'buyer pool' of the first 100 potential buyers is probably quite well educated in terms of values in your area. These buyers have all seen every home on the market and only view fresh homes on the market, or perhaps one they originally showed interest in that has dropped its price.

In the first ten days of marketing, you will get all of the 100 buyers in your 'buyer pool' looking at your ad or sign on the lawn and some of them will come and view your home if they perceive it is in their price range. Great stuff! Activity on your home!

If they don't buy it at that point, for whatever reason, your only 'buyer pool' left is the new buyer coming into the market.

That covers the first two or three weeks of marketing.

I hope you followed the logic there because it is quite important to you when you set the price on your home.

The most common mistake vendors make when pricing their home is setting the price too high on day one on the understanding that "We can always drop it down later". Your biggest pool of buyers will be looking at your ad and your price on day one and will not even walk through your door! They know it is too dear because of their experience. So by setting your price too high you have automatically lost 75% of your potentially largest group of buyers and committed yourself to probably an extra three months on the market!

The buyer interest in your home is usually at its peak in the first two weeks it is exposed to the market. You may get ten times the buyer activity in the first two weeks of market exposure. When you drop your price three weeks into the marketing, you have already missed the boat with your 'buyer pool' of 100 buyers and now you are limited to a trickle of interest. Don't blame the Salesperson!

Please realise this fact as a fact. Only one buyer in 1,000 that walks through your door is not aware of the local house values. You have a one in 1000 chance that yours is the first home they have walked into, they have no idea of values and that that one buyer in 1000 may fall in love with your home and pay your 'over the top' price. That is only one buyer in 1,000!

The other 999 buyers have all walked in and said to themselves, or the Salesperson, "They have to be joking on their price don't they?" So on the one in 1000 chance of an idiot buying your home you risk turning away another 999 solid buyers.

Get it on the market at the right price on day one and let the Salesperson do the rest. You are looking for $200,000 aren't you? Put it on for no more than $210,000 and be prepared to be reasonably firm when you negotiate!

Mike, the salesperson, asks for some Dollars from you, towards the Advertising.

Well he was a little subtler than that. He used phrases like 'lifting your profile' or 'Maximum market impact on day one'.

From an Agent's viewpoint, as opposed to a Salesperson, there is only so much money that can be put into advertising a property. Think about it this way. If we sell only half of our listings and our advert budget is $100,000 per year it means that each year we are throwing away approx $50,000 in advertising that we will never recoup. On the day your listing comes into my office, I, as the person paying for all the advertising, have no idea if your home is saleable. I have no idea whether you will keep your home on the market or if you will withdraw it when you realise you will not get your high price. I will, therefore, lose any dollars I, as the Agent, may spend on your home. On the law of averages though, I will commit to a certain level of advertising for every listing. I have to do that to keep sales staff wanting to work for my office.

Let me put this viewpoint to you. No matter how much or how little is spent on advertising your home; it will not, or is very unlikely to, increase the price of your home! While there are comparable properties for sale in your location, no one is going to pay the dollars for the 2012 Cadillac when it is obvious they are buying a Nissan compact.

Increasing the advertising profile for your property is always aimed at speeding up the sale rather than upping the price.

More inside trade info. Here for you to consider.

After paying franchise fees and Salesperson's commissions, the amount of commission left to the Agent is between 40% and 42% of the total commission. As a rule of thumb, most agencies spend 10% of their turnover on advertising. That 10% of income is the equivalent of 25% of their nett operating cash flow after paying Salespeople and franchise fees.

Another point to consider is that if I advertise your home today, I have to pay that advert bill in maybe 30 days. I probably won't receive any commission for the sale of your home for at least 75 days and that is only if your home sells reasonably quickly or sells at all!

Here is another item for you to think about. All the Real Estate Offices are in an advertising war because the public have bought into the idea that the Office with the biggest ads is the most successful. If the office down the road has the biggest adverts, the public has the perception that they are the biggest and best. *The reality is more likely to be that their team of Salespeople are the best at getting advertising contributions from their vendors!!*

If you are keen to get a speedier sale then make a contribution to the advertising. If you are only willing to sell if you 'get your price' don't expect your dollars to increase the sale price.

Okay, you have signed up for three months exclusively at $215,000 with Salesperson Mike from ABC Realty. As we said earlier, your agency is not with Mike, it is with ABC Realty.
What happens next?

One of your comments to Mike was that you wanted communication from him frequently!

What happens when you sign up with the Agent

Within the next two or three days, the sign should appear on your front lawn in as prominent a place as possible.

Mike will have gone back to the office and processed your listing, which includes

- Writing out 2 or 3 adverts- Run on ads, Open homes, Flyers etc
- Taking Photos of the home.
- Organising a time to bring the rest of his team to view your home
- Organising an open home schedule for the next three weeks
- Advising all other offices in his group of your home being on the market.
- Putting your paperwork into the office system/computer so your home appears along with all the other listings the office holds.
- Organising a window card for the Office window display.
  - Organising the Internet advertisement. Etc etc etc.

When the paper war has been won, Mike should then be trawling his file of past unsatisfied buyers (remember we talked about the 'buyer pool'?) to see if he can get anyone interested in viewing your home urgently.

Over the next few days Mike should be calling you and keeping you updated on his activities. He should be bringing the sales team to view your home all together. He can then talk to the team collectively and explain the main features of the home, introduce them to you as the vendors etc. After the team has been through you should get some feedback from Mike as to the team's thoughts on your property and its price.

A number of Mike's colleagues bring clients through to view your home. Mike asked you to make yourself scarce when clients were in the home. The reason for this is that people are generally very polite and will not wish to offend you by saying that your wallpaper is ghastly, or the second bedroom smells etc.. If you are not present, they *will* say those remarks to the Salesperson. The Salesperson needs to hear those remarks to be able to judge the buyers' interest levels. When Salespeople hear negative comments, they realise that it can be the first sign of buyer interest!

At the end of the viewing they can ask the buyer their thoughts on the property. If they comment that they like it but the wallpaper is poor, that gives the Salesperson the chance to start closing the sale. Perhaps by saying "it would only cost a couple of thousand to repaper the house, would you be interested in making an offer to buy the home for that couple of thousand below their asking price?"

Most sales start with a negative comment that the well trained Salesperson can turn into a positive. So, from a Salesperson's point of view we need to hear those negatives and we won't get them if you are around!

Mike gets back to you with the feedback from those Salespeople and although you don't get any offers, the feedback is such that we think we are on the market at a good price. Always listen to the feedback. Sometimes it can be a very small thing that puts a buyer completely off the home.

As an example, in a home unit I was selling, I had a well presented home that was well priced and in a good location but it would not sell. After 5 weeks the price was reduced and, like a good salesperson should, I contacted all the people that had been through to tell them of the price drop. The first lady I rang could not recall the address so I described the house to her. Then she made the comment "Oh yes, the snake House!" Only then did it become clear. Just inside one of the bedroom doors was a four-foot high stuffed cobra snake (I kid you not) ready to strike. Several people had commented on the thing at Open homes but I had not picked up on their words. As soon as people walked in, the first thing they saw was this damn snake and it immediately put them into a concerned or negative state of mind. So, no sale.

I rang the vendor and suggested we move the snake to a friend's home. Two days later we had a sale! To the first buyer through the home after the snake had been removed. Maybe it was a coincidence. Maybe it was my fault for not picking it up earlier. But by listening to the feedback we got a sale, which was the main objective.

Another big turn off for buyers is to walk up the drive and have a big dog come tearing out of the house and barking madly. I don't care how lovable the dog is when he gets to know you. Once the buyers are into a mindset of concern, they won't relax so you can scrub the home off the list. So for the sake of the sale we try and remove vendors, stuffed snakes and dogs. I am sure we can add to the list of things we want to keep away from buyers things like noisy or arguing or crying children, loud TV and stereos, sinks full of dirty dishes, laundries full of dirty washing etc.

Let's spend a couple of lines here working out the buyer mentality as they make a purchasing decision.

The Buyer Mentality

When you buy, say, a car you want some things as a minimum. Let's say 4 wheels, 4 doors, seating, 2-litre engine etc. Logically you should buy something like a 2005 Skoda or a Lada car. Yet you don't buy Skoda or Lada, you buy the latest

Japanese cars with all the bells and whistles such as air conditioning, CD players, electric windows etc etc.

What you have here is a classic example of needs versus wants. What you need could be satisfied with a 2005 Skoda. That is a logical and cost effective decision to make. Your wants are more emotional. You want the comfort or prestige of the latest Toyota or Cadillac and you want it as new as you can get it. When you go to the car yard, the salesperson always gets you to sit inside the new car. Smell the new car smell. Operate the electric windows. Turn on the CD player. You sit in the car and use all your senses to take in the features of this new motorcar, your new motorcar! Touch it, smell it, see it, feel it! You imagine yourself zapping over to the beach in summer with the air conditioning on full. The salesperson is appealing to all your emotional needs and trying to get you to move away from the cold hard reality of logic that says you only need the 2005 Skoda!

When I have a buyer in the home, I want to appeal to her emotion by showing her the big gleaming kitchen. She can see herself whipping up some super meal in her mind's eye in this culinary palace and being like the Supermom they show in the adverts on the TV. What I don't want to do is to remind her that a big kitchen takes a lot more cleaning. The very presence of a sink full of dishes will bring her out of her reverie back to the cold hard fact that she will still have to do the dishes! Emotional bliss is replaced by cold logic and the sale is often gone!

People buy on emotion and justify with logic. It's true in 95% of all people and that's a fact. Ever heard the saying "You don't buy the sausage, you buy the sizzle!". Ever seen a sausage ad with just a packet of sausages. You only see sausages in adverts that are in the frying pan and sizzling away merrily. You can almost smell them cooking can't you? Are you focussing on the logic of the ground up low-quality meat packed in a thin latex-like covering that feels rather unpleasant to the touch? Or are you remembering how they smell when they start sizzling. Perhaps you are recalling the picnic last summer when you tossed a few bangers on the barby and your association of the sausages is that of warm summer days round the barby? Is your dominant buying motive based on the logic or the emotion?

Put the emotion/logic equation to work. You have a choice of buying two sets of shoes. One is dull and boring and logical. The other is more exciting in colour and $15 dearer. You want the dearer shoes! You justify the emotional decision to buy the dearer shoes with the logic of "Yes, they are dearer but they would probably go with more of my wardrobe wouldn't they?"

In a housing context, you want a 3-bedroom home with a single garage. They are available in some parts of town with a price of $110,000. Yet you have seen this one home that you have fallen in love with at $130.000 and you justify the extra cost with the logic of "and it is so much closer to school for the children" Is it $20,000 closer to the school or does it just "feel" nicer?

Next time you go shopping for something that is a discretionary item, check on your thought processes. Do you buy on emotion and justify the purchase with logic?

Getting back to the mad dogs barking and the stuffed snake etc. Unless you are relaxed, you will not allow yourself the indulgence of emotional feeling. Without the emotional and 'warm fuzzies' feeling, the sale is not even in the frame.

Investment buyers are generally the only buyers that will look at the property as a collection of building materials and not be concerned with the emotion of the property at all. They view the property as an investment that has to return a certain percentage after costs. That percentage is usually 3% or 4% above the current mortgage rate. The income is dependent on what they will be able to achieve as a weekly rental figure. Back in the early 1990's when mortgages were running at a 12% interest rate the Investors were looking for a 15% return. With the high interest rates, there were a few desperate vendors who had to take whatever an investor buyer would offer and a few investors became quite wealthy around that time.

OPEN HOMES

Ok. It's time for the first open home. What do you have to do?

Ideally you should clean the home from top to toe and have a major session in the garden. Weed. Mow the lawns. Tidy the garage. As suggested earlier we want to paint a picture of the ideal home for our buyers. We want them to walk inside the home and make it so easy for them to picture themselves entertaining their friends around the barbecue. Playing pool in the games room, whipping up a super meal in the kitchen.

What we don't want to do is remind them that, with a quarter acre section they would need to spend a half-day per fortnight mowing the lawn. Etc.

If I may be so bold here, why not pay out $100 or so to one of those domestic cleaning services and get them to come in and give the whole house a good spring-cleaning. Pay someone else to come in and rip round the garden. Once the main clean and tidy up has been done, it is fairly easy to keep the home and garden clean and tidy. The new look should more than be repaid by a speedier sale. No guarantees but it should make the home more appealing to buyers.

Before the open home, make sure all the dishes are cleaned and tidied away, magazines tidy, beds made etc. Have a couple of quality magazines lying on the coffee table in the same way they do in the home and garden magazines. You are trying to present an image here. It's called marketing!

Put some air freshener through the home. Have a pot of coffee bubbling away on the stove. Open some windows to let the fresh air in. If you have net curtains or blinds, pull them right back to let the maximum amount of daylight flood in to your home. Put away or hide all small portable items of value or jewellery. It is only a precaution but one that is well worth taking.

When you have prepared everything as well as you can, go away from the home. Completely away from the home. Drive into town and have coffee at a kerbside café. Don't be tempted to just park up the road and count how many people come to your open home. At the best, it is depressing if nobody comes. At the worst, you look a real dork to all the neighbours.

What will Mike be doing at the open home?

He will be near the front door ready to greet the people as they come in. He will offer them a brochure on your property and ask them for their contact details   (Name and Phone Number etc). If he is not inundated with people he may give them a guided tour of the home and point out all the features of the home. If he is busy with lots of people coming in, he may just restrict himself to staying by the front door and telling the visitors to make sure they look at, for instance, the new bathroom.. He should have all alternative exits locked securely so that all the prospective buyers have to exit by walking past him again. At his point he can ask them for any feedback on the home and gauge their interest levels on your home.

From your open home Mike will probably pick up a few buyers that he can show other homes to. Don't be offended. It may well be that a buyer from another open home will be shown your home.

At the end of the first open home try and grab a couple of minutes with Mike the Salesperson. This is usually the first time we can examine the marketing situation after offering the home to the public.

I always worked along the line that the vendors and I were a team. So I always used the phrase "WE have a problem" rather than 'you have a problem.'

Here is the rundown on the marketing situation.

Nobody came through the Open Home.
WE have a problem! Unless there is some major local event that draws away our client base, why did nobody come through the home? Poorly written advert? Advert too small? Price too high? Suggestion- Try another open home next week with a new advert and at a different time of day.

100 people came to the Open home and nobody showed interest.
WE have a problem! The buyers that did come through did not perceive the home as good value? There may be a major drawback in the home that a number of the buyers commented on. Suggestion- fix the fault or fix the price.

Only the neighbours came.
That is not a problem. The neighbours will tell their friends and that is all more advertising for you that is free! Suggestion- as in the first situation. New advert and a different time of day for the next open home. Either way, you have now exposed your home to the public and you should now be able to have some idea of how the public perceives your home.

All the people that came through commented that the price was too high

WE have a problem! Probably only a couple of people commented on the price but it is still feedback you need to hear. Suggestion – Adjust the price. Maybe consider a Price band of $200,000 to $220,000.

Mike has one buyer showing some interest.

Mike will be doing the follow up that night and should be getting back to you in the next 24 hours with some feedback.

Mike will be highlighting your property to his colleagues at the weekly sales meeting. Occasionally at our meetings I would ask each Salesperson to highlight one of their listings only and ask the rest of the team why it has not sold. That feedback was then given to the vendor. Another trick we used at our meetings was to highlight one listing per Salesperson and then run a competition to get that listing sold within 30 days. There would usually be a small prize for the first of those listings to get a deal on it. Another trick we tried was to have a list of each Salespersons top three vendors by way of their motivation to sell and the pricing on their properties. Always we were trying to highlight the listings that were saleable by being well priced or with a highly motivated vendor.

Mike should be reporting back to you on at least a weekly basis. In our office, those reports had to be written and posted out by Tuesday. Every two or three weeks each Salesperson had to have a face to face marketing review meeting with each vendor where those weekly reports were laid on the table and discussed. After every second market review meeting there had to be some change to the listing. That change could be to the price or the style of marketing or a contribution to an increased advert profile. From my point of view as the Agent, I felt that if we had been marketing the property for six weeks with no success, we had to change something. The old saying that "If nothing Changes, then nothing Changes!" is so very true when selling homes.

The marketing of your home continues on and eventually it will sell. Whether it takes two months or even two years is usually over to the vendors and their willingness to meet the market. Imagine, if you will, any product you purchase irregularly, like a car. You have not bought one for three years and you are horrified at the prices they are asking. You went back to the car yard where you bought your last car from three years ago and their prices were high. So you shopped around. Once you had done the rounds of all the local caryards you got some idea of current values and probably made a buying decision.

*An **educated** buying decision.*

It's the same with houses. Prices go up, so you shop around until you get educated and then make a decision. Whatever happens, you don't pay over the odds in price do you? Well, until your home is well priced, no one will pay over the odds for your home either.

Points to remember:
- *There is only one buyer in a thousand who is not educated on local house prices.*
- *The other 999 comparison-shopped and know what your home is worth.*
- *Your home is only worth what someone else will pay for it.*
- *There isn't a Salesperson in the industry who can change that!*
- *Of course, if you are willing to wait for that thousandth buyer?*

Chapter 5 - you have a keen buyer!

So, after one day, or one week, or one year of being on the market, you get a phone call from Mike to say he wants to see both you and your partner together, as he has an offer on your home and he needs to discuss it urgently. Your immediate reaction is "How much are they offering?" Most salespersons with some experience will not tell you the price at this point. If you know the price before the meeting you may be very negative about it and as Mike will explain to you later, price is only ever one component of the offer you are receiving.

Price is only one part of the Offer

Remember that phrase and don't get too hung up on the price when you are shown the agreement. There are any numbers of ways to sweeten the deal or make the price more acceptable to both sides

Discussing the offer from the buyer

Make a time as soon as possible to sit down together. If at all possible, have the meeting in your home or your office. If you go to Mike's office you are already at a psychological disadvantage. Trust me on this one, ok! Be fair to Mike and have all the owners of the property at the meeting so you can make a decision.

When you sit down with Mike, he should have enough copies of the offer for everyone to read while he explains all the components of the offer. You should be told about the purchasers, Mike's estimate of their ability to complete the purchase, the amount of deposit they want to put down, the settlement date they require, the chattels they want included in the sale, any conditions that the contract is subject to (Finance, Valuation, house sale, builder report etc) and finally the price they are offering. The reason the offer is presented in this way is that most vendors will only be concerned about the price and there may well be other factors in the offer you want changing so we will discuss them first. Later we will go over some of the conditions and explain them to you in more detail.

As this is for illustration only, let's assume that this is an offer for cash and the offer is for $194,000. There are no extra conditions attached and everything else in the offer is acceptable to you, but you are adamant you want the $200,000 or no deal!

Let's look at the big picture here. If you have only been on the market for a couple of days you could be forgiven for being optimistic that you will get your $200,000. If you have been on the market for 12 months and this is the first offer you have received you should perhaps be treating the offer with a little more respect. Tell Mike that you want more and *ask how he thinks we should go about getting the purchaser to up his offer.* Your legal position here is that you have a buyer willing to commit to buying your home for $194,000. He/they have made a formal offer and signed that offer. If all the owners of the property sign to accept the offer then both sides of the contract are legally bound to perform and finish the contract. Within reason, the buyer is bound to his offer until you or they indicate the offer is cancelled or not accepted. That is a very simple statement of your legal position and a lawyer would probably give you a couple of extra pages of heretofore's etc. But your signature binds you when both parties sign.

Here is the down side to you. The instant you alter the offer by, for instance, deleting $194,000 and inserting $200,000 the buyer has no further legal obligations to you or to the offer. Be aware before making any alterations to the offer that you may be kissing off the only potential buyer for your home so far!

Ask Mike what he thinks they will go to. It may be that the buyer is working with another of the Salespeople in Mike's office and Mike is not aware of their financial ability or their enthusiasm for your home. However he may have some indication that they are pretty keen to buy it so it is always worth pumping Mike for whatever info he has got.

Try and remember that Mike is acting as a go between for both you and the Purchaser. He has to remain neutral to both parties. He cannot favour one side over the other, as he could be held liable in the event of a dispute. Often, when the negotiating gets to a tense stage, Mike will also be acting as the referee!

It is always a gamble when you get an offer on your home and you want a few more dollars. Unless I had been told by the other Salesperson that this was the highest they would go to, I would usually recommend that my vendors have at least one go at counter offering on the price. Towards the end of this book we will go into some negotiating tactics. For this stage we only need to look at the mechanics of the sale rather than the tactics and games of negotiating.

Counter Offering

To make a counteroffer the process is quite simple. Make sure that everything else is acceptable to you and then strike out the price of $194,000 and insert $200,000 or $202,000 or whatever figure you want to put in. Write your figure in as both a number and in words. Place your initials next to the alteration and sign the agreement as the vendor(s).

Mike will now go back to see the buyers and see if he can get them to agree to your price or at least come closer to it than they started with.

To accept your price, the buyers have only to place their initials alongside the alterations to accept them and the contract is now binding again on all parties. They may counter offer back to you at $198,000 and so forth until you both have agreed on the price. The main thing to remember here is that at any time one party can back away from the agreement until both parties sign the agreement and initial their approval to every alteration to all copies of the contract. When that happens, the other party cannot just delete their last alteration to make the agreement binding again. The offer will be at an end and you have lost the buyer and probably got Mike a little teed off as his commission sailed out of the door when you could not agree on a price.

Dates mean dollars

As I stated earlier, price is just one part of the offer to purchase. Too many people get hung up on price alone, or let their ego get in the way because they feel insulted at the low offer received. Always keep in the back of your mind, that an alteration of a settlement date by, say, two months could allow the buyers to save up another two or three thousand to get nearer to your hoped for price. Maybe if they need to be in by a certain day, they should pay another thousand to you for the inconvenience of you moving out quickly or having to move to temporary accommodation until your home is ready. Maybe they don't need the home for three months, why not get them to settle early and let you stay on as tenants at a peppercorn rental? That could add up to another thousand dollars or so that you make on the deal. There's usually more than one way to sweeten a deal if your Salesperson is on the ball.

Let's go through the deal to the end before we start talking about other conditions etc that complicate most agreements. Remember that we are talking in *general* terms for a variety of states or countries. The contract process will alter in different countries slightly.

When the deal is signed copies of the agreement are given to each party and to each party's solicitors. The purchasers' solicitors order a 'Title search'. The Title', or more correctly called "Certificate of Title" acts similarly to the Logbook of your car. It confirms you are the owner of the Property. It also states who else has an interest in the property, like the banks that lent you the money to buy in the first place etc. The title also gives information about things like right of ways and easements etc., any compulsory purchase orders etc. The solicitor usually has up to 15 working days to come up with any problems on the title, which could be sufficiently serious to warrant cancelling the sale.

The vendors' solicitor finds out how much the vendors owe the bank or the council for rates etc and advises all parties with a registered interest in the property that you are selling and they are to advise him of the amount of their interest to be satisfied on the day the sale occurs.

You will be called in to sign the transfer papers and other than that, for the most part the solicitor takes care of the legal side of the sale.

Sounds pretty simple? Leave it to the solicitor to handle. It is worth their fee for the peace of mind.

Deposit

Before we get to the sale being completed, the buyer usually has to pay a deposit. In the days gone by, the buyer was obliged to pay a 10% deposit. That has all changed and it is not that rare for buyers to pay little or no deposit at all ***provided that was what was called for in the agreement.*** The Agent or his Salesperson is obliged to collect the deposit within three days of the contract being signed and that deposit is then held in the Agent's trust account. Usually, once the agreement is unconditional the deposit can be released to the vendor's solicitor if the Agent has held it for at least 10 days. The Agent takes their commission out at this point and pays the Salespeople. The Salesperson will usually ask for 6% to 10% as deposit in an agreement as it means they will get paid promptly rather than waiting for the sale to settle and then for your Solicitor to pay them out.

Contracts – details and fishhooks

Let's go through the agreement form and look for some fishhooks.

1) At the top of the page is a space for the date. This should only be filled in when the last signature or set of initials is placed on the form to make it a binding agreement. There are clauses in the small print that say things like …"from the 15th day after the signing of this agreement".. so let's get that date accurate.

2) Full names and address please for the vendors and purchasers. 'Mr and Mrs J Smith' will not identify you sufficiently.

3) Full street address please. Include suburb and town.

4) Full Legal Description in as much detail as possible, especially where we are selling units or cross lease properties.

5) Purchase price in words as well as numbers. All alterations to be adequately deleted sufficient to leave no doubt in the mind of any legal eagle.

6) Deposit. How much, when it is to be paid, who is to hold it and where.

7) Settlement date. Make it a weekday, as Solicitors don't work weekends. Possession day may be different from Settlement date. If it is different, note it here.

8) Builders report wanted? Allow at least 15 days for the report to be obtained and read. Anything less than that and you may have an unenforceable contract.

9) Chattels. There is not enough space to define the difference between fixtures and fittings as "Chattels". If in doubt, put it in. If it is excluded from the sale, write in "Main bedroom chandelier not included". Leave no doubt in anyone's mind.

10) Finance condition. How much, Being borrowed from who or which bank. Loan to be confirmed by what date?

11) Other conditions page.
There are any number of conditions you can add to a contract. You could insert a condition to the effect that the agreement is subject to you winning the big Prize at this weekend's Lotto draw. If the other party accepts the condition

you have an agreement. In reality there are usually only 5 types of Condition in any residential property sale.

Those 5 are:-

1   Subject to house sale
Included in this clause should be the address of the house for sale. The amount the buyer will take for the house he wants to sell and when it has to be sold by. Ask Mike if he knows the property and it's approx value. What are his thoughts on the properties saleability?

2   Escape clause
Usually put in with a 'subject to house sale' clause. Effectively you are taking your home off the market while the buyer tries to sell his home or raise the finance. This clause allows you to continue marketing your home and if you get another offer, the first buyer has 3 or 5 days in which to go unconditional or withdraw his offer so you can proceed with the second offer.

3   Subject to Specialist report.
This condition allows the buyer to have a builder or some other specialist (valuer, electrician etc) access to the home to answer questions that the buyer may have. This clause may have an extra in the printing that should the specialist find anything untoward the deal may be cancelled. Usually the wording is to the

effect that the buyer has to be satisfied with the report or he can pull out. It is a little vague and favours the buyer but it is still a common clause in agreements.

4 Subject to Solicitors approval.
This clause is the vaguest of all. In its correct form, the clause should read "subject to the Solicitors approval as to the form and content of this agreement". More often than not, it is left very vaguely worded and the solicitor can disapprove of the purchase because he doesn't like the area or the neighbours or anything the buyer tells him to disapprove of. It is very biased towards the buyer and gives the solicitor too much say.

5 Subject to having suitable zoning.
Not quite so common but the buyer may want to extend the home or use it as a home office or something similar. The buyer needs to check out the local zoning before committing to the purchase.

If you have any doubts about the agreement, please satisfy the doubt **before** you sign the agreement. Ask the salesperson or your solicitor. They are there to help you!

Points to remember:
- *Price is only ever one part of the Offer.*
- *Dates can mean dollars.*
- *Always read the small print.*
- *If in doubt, take professional advice!*

Chapter 6 - What can a Salesperson expect from a Buyer?

Shouldn't this be the other way round?

Well maybe it should be the other way round, but let's look at what a salesperson is looking for in a buyer. Buyers and sellers tend to forget that the salesperson is a businessman or an investor who is investing in himself with time and training. He wants a return on that investment. Let's face it; Salespeople *need* a return on that investment so they can put food on his or her table! Just as an investor in the share market picks out the stocks he thinks will give him a return or profit on his investment of money, the Salesperson has to look at Buyers as potential returns on the investment of his time and efforts. If that sounds a little cynical, it is exactly the same relationship that you have with any businessperson. They deal with you to get a profit out of you. I don't know of any single businessman that is dealing with you to make a loss! Think about it, reader. All I have done is put it down in writing!

Recent changes in Consumer legislation have added to the buyer's safeguards. Not so long ago Real Estate Salesperson, for the most part, had their main responsibility to the vendor. It is only relatively recently that Salespeople had to give serious and statutory thought also to the best interests of the buyer.

Ever wondered who paid the wages of the Salesperson? It is the vendor!

In the contract of agency between the vendor and the Real Estate Office the vendor is called the 'Principal' and the buyers should remember that relationship.

Go with this scenario. You want to purchase a new home. You want a three-bedroom home with double garaging. A second living area would be an advantage. The section doesn't need to be too big but you do need room to park your boat off the street. Maximum price you want to spend is $190,000.

Now correct me if your experience differs from mine here. But if you went out with a variety of Salespeople and were shown 100 homes. How many of those 100 homes would fill all or pretty much most of your stated requirements? 20? 15? Or less?
Why do Salespeople waste your time and their petrol taking you to homes that don't come even half way to meeting your needs?

Here is the worst thing about your time wasting trips. They show you homes on the market at prices up to $230,000. You finally find one you like and it is on the market at $225,000! You put in your offer of $190,000 and they counter offer at $220,000. Depressed? You should be!

Whose fault is it?

Sorry to say but it is the fault (for the most part) of the buyers before you!
There is a saying in Real Estate that they (unofficially) teach in Real Estate training courses. That saying is……..

All buyers are liars (and all vendors are benders of the truth!)

Hard to hear?

Unfortunately it is true. We listen all day to buyers and sellers that tell us this or that and we know full well that what they are saying is what they believe they want or what they will buy *today* if the price is right. If the buyer has uninformed or unreasonable expectations they will quickly discover they cannot get what they want for the money they want to pay. Often, when the buyer has been out with a couple of Salespeople their buying parameters change. Unfortunately, the buyers do not always go back to the first two Salespeople. To counter this, Salespeople will often show the buyers a couple of homes that are slightly outside the buyers stated wants to check out whether the buyer is quoting 'needs' or' wants'.

If I am an obedient Salesperson and I listen to your stated needs, I may have six homes to show you up to $195,000 asking price. I may spend three or four hours trotting you round those homes and not satisfy you. When I hear you have bought something in a suburb that you told me you would not touch and at a price of $207,500, I am (justifiably, I feel) less than pleased!

Qualifying the Buyer

It did not take me long, as a salesperson, to take on board the "All buyers are liars" saying. I added the bit about vendors myself. Don't get uptight. It is quite correct when I say that a lot of the practises taken on by Real Estate Salespeople are only to help them overcome some of the practises we come up against from our clients.

Now, when a buyer comes to see me with a list of requirements, I first check how many properties we hold that have most or all of the needs of the buyer. Then I go through those properties with the buyer before I put the buyer in my car. At this point I want to ask the buyer three separate lines of questions.

Firstly I ask them how many of their requirements are absolute *needs* and which of them are only *wants*. For instance, they may ask for a double garage. They may only need a single garage but need extra space for a ride-on mower etc. So another property that has a single garage with a sizeable garden shed can now go on our viewing list.

The second type of question always starts with the words "Are you open to....?" For example, 'Are you open to looking in different areas if you can't find what you want in your preferred suburb?' 'Are you open to spending in excess of your stated $190,000 if you I show you something a little dearer that possibly has all your requirements?'

Running buyers around is time consuming, expensive and not always productive. You find the buyers the perfect home and for some reason they are not able to purchase. Which leads me to my third and most important question, which is...

'If we can find the home you like today, what position are you in to make an offer to purchase that home today?'

It is a hard question to ask but it is probably the one question that separates the top achievers from the under achievers!

A, B and C Buyers

This is crunch time.

I classify buyers into 3 categories. A, B or C.

Using the analogy we used at the beginning of this chapter, the Share market investor does not take every available stock into his portfolio. He selects only the ones he believes he has a reasonable chance of making a profit on. That seems reasonable doesn't it? So why should the Real Estate salesperson waste his time and expertise on people who he knows will have no chance of giving him any return on his investment with them? Yes I know it sounds very cynical but it's a very practical and professional way of doing business, if you think about it. We are no different than your Doctor, Dentist, Dairy owner etc. Ever thought of it like that?

Back to the buyers and how I graded mine. I believe this is a very commonly used formula but I'm only being honest about my own practises and making no claims about how other Salesperson work.

- A category **A** buyer is *Ready, Willing and Able* to make a buying decision today.
- A category **B** buyer is only able to meet 2 of the above 3 requirements. They may be ready and willing to buy but are not able to make a buying decision if they see something they like. Perhaps they still have a home to sell.
- A category **C** buyer is only able to meet 1 of the above requirements.

A category **A** buyer will get my full attention. If we can't meet their needs, they will get a daily phone call from me advising them of all new stock coming in and also I will be checking that their selection criteria has not changed and that they have not purchased with another company or decided not to move home etc.

A category **B** buyer will get my limited attention only after I have checked what they need to do to become an A category buyer. If their home needs to be sold, can we market it for them? If it is already on the market I will give them some suggestions to increase its marketability. Maybe they don't need to sell and can use the equity in their own home to buy the new home and keep the old one as a rental investment. I will follow up once weekly with a category B buyer to check that their situation remains unchanged.

A category **C** buyer, I'm sorry to say, gets virtually no activity from me. They may want to buy but are unable to, because they owe too much on their home and they have lost their job etc. I keep in contact with them maybe once a month. That may sound harsh but I usually spend some time with them at the interview advising them how they can improve their situation by maybe refinancing their existing home or extending it as a cheaper option than buying new.

If I sound a little mercenary here, follow my logic. I am still putting in my 14/7. I am running and paying for a near new $49,000 car and all other associated costs and I am a busy and successful Salesperson. In five years of selling homes I only ever received one complaint and that complaint was a little strange as I got between a husband and wife in an argument over a buying decision. I suggested they both back off and think about it, over night, as the house would still be there tomorrow. I wasn't closing on the sale but was reported to my manager as being pushy! Go Figure!

Why should I waste my car and time running round with people, making convenient times with vendors and raising their hopes needlessly when there is zero chance of any sale possibly happening? Remember we talked earlier about the comparison with the Share market investor? Can you see it a little clearer know?

Put it into another context. Would any other trade or profession you can think of put in 10 or 15 hours of their time at totally no cost to the 'customer' without asking themselves first 'what were the chances of making any money to pay for my time and expenses?'

I am not a perfectionist by any stretch of the imagination, but by studying hard for 3 years at my own expense and taking and passing all the exams available, I hold the qualification that ranked me among the top 15% of all Real Estate Salespeople in terms of knowing my job inside and out. I was not a taxi driver or a tour guide. I was a professional Real Estate Salesperson and proud of it!

If, however, I took you out to view homes, you were taken only to homes that were close to your stated price range and had most if not all of the requirements you asked for. I rarely showed more than 6 homes to a buyer on one day as quite often you got a good read on their personal tastes after showing them through the first 2 homes. I rarely took a buyer out more than three times to view homes. If they had not made a purchasing decision by the time I had shown them 12 or 15 homes it was obvious I was not reading them correctly for their needs. Also it was not very often we had more than 15 homes in any one category to show to a buyer.

Some of the customers that walked into the office were priceless. The following are true stories.

One customer walked in and wanted to look at all homes in the range $90 to $100,000. I was very new at this point and bundled him into my car without asking the qualifying questions. After showing him everything we had on our books, we got back to the office four hours later. I tried to close him on any of the properties. It was only then I discovered he was from 'down country and he had recently had his house valued at $92,000 and wanted to compare it with houses in our town so he could go back and argue with his valuer!

Another client was a little old lady who walked into the Office with her shopping bags and wanted to be shown a property in one of the suburbs. Naturally I was keen and loaded her and her shopping into the car (You can see it coming can't you?). I drove her up to the property. She got out of the car. Took one look at the house and said she did not like the look of it. Then she told me not to bother taking her back to the Office as she only lived 3 doors up the road! She would walk from here! When I got back to the Office, I admit I was a little angered that I was, literally, taken for a ride. The others in the Office were howling with laughter. She was always pulling that stunt and looked at the window outside for the newest Salesperson on the team to work her trick with.

The worst one of all was the little old dear who got Bruce from our office (not me this time) to take her 52 km out of town to look at a house in the country. When she got there, she told Bruce she did not like it. But not to worry as her mate lived next door and she would run her home later. Bruce (good on him!) bundled the old beggar back into his car and drove her back to town and dumped her at the bus station. She complained to the Manager about Bruce. Bruce had already quit the industry within an hour of his return.

Be Prepared as a Buyer- Needs versus wants.

Right, let's get back to your role as a Prospective buyer.

If you want to get the best value from your Salesperson, be honest and be open with him/her.
Before you even contemplate ringing up a Salesperson, work out why you are moving. Get all the family members involved in a round table discussion and get some agreement between you on the main features you _need_ in your new home. 3 bedrooms (2 double and 1 single) double garage (or single with large workshop). Do you want a completely redecorated home or would you prefer one you can decorate yourself (saves you money and it will end up being decorated to your taste).

Then compile a list of _wants_. An extra bedroom or living area would be a bonus rather than a necessity so that is a want rather than a need. Handy to schools would be a want rather than a need. Alarm system could be a bonus. An outdoor living/Barbecue area would be a want rather than a need.

As a final preparation before calling the Real Estate Offices, go and see your bank manager or mortgage broker to see how much you will be allowed to borrow or how much of your earnings you want to commit to a mortgage.

Let the Salesperson do the best job for you

When you do call the Salesperson, you can be fairly firm in what you want to be looking for in your next home and how much you want to spend as a maximum.

Don't be too afraid to tell your Salesperson what you want. If you don't get on with him/her when you have been shown a few homes, it is simple enough to not make any more appointments with him and then use another Salesperson instead. The more information you can give to the Salesperson, the more help he can be to you!

If you don't like a property he shows you, tell him you don't like it and if possible, tell him why. Maybe the lounge is too small, kitchen too dated, grounds too big, décor too tatty, area too rough. If you can give him a clue, two things may happen. Firstly he may have a idea that could transform the home into exactly what you want and secondly, he won't waste your time taking you to the homes on his list that offer the same features that you don't like in this home.

Let's take a quick look at some of the reasons you don't like the home and see if there are possibly some ways to overcome those problems. Where your concern is about the state of the décor or the tiredness of the fixtures and fittings etc it may well be that the vendor has already made an adjustment in their asking price to allow for the deficiency and may not be willing to drop their price by a huge amount as they feel it is already priced for the market. However, you won't know if you don't ask!

The lounge is too small.
Do you need a large lounge? Is there a second living area that could be used as a family room? The small lounge could then be used as a quieter area away from the noisy kids etc.

Kitchen too dated.
If the price was dropped by, say, $8,000 you could upgrade the kitchen to a newer style.

Grounds too big,
Are the grounds big enough to subdivide or cross lease? If you could get somewhere between $30,000 and $50,000 for selling off the back of the section, would that be an equitable way to reduce the cost of the house?

Décor too tatty.
Reduce the price of your offer by $5,000 and redecorate the whole house to your own taste.

Area too rough.
Not a lot we can do with the neighbourhood. Why is it too rough? If it is too close to the park, is that not also a plus because you can keep an eye on the kids?

Those are some suggestions that most buyers never think of when they first view homes. They are, quite rightly, looking for the best value and the ideal home for them. Often, they don't see the potential in a home. If the buyer is keeping quiet about why they don't like the home, the Salesperson cannot be of any help and, more importantly, you are not getting the best value from the Salesperson.

The Salesperson may show you perhaps six to ten homes in one session. At the end of the trip, you will be totally confused unless you take some notes. At the end of each home inspection, I would ask the buyer for their thoughts on the home they had viewed. What did they like and what did they dislike? I would generally make a note on the back of the listing sheet. Firstly to be able to recap at the end of the trip and secondly to be able to give some feedback to the vendor. Often during the trip they would pass a negative comment about a home (small bedrooms) and I could remind them that at the first or second house they were quite impressed with the bedroom sizes. Before we got back into the car after viewing the last home on the list, I would review with them all the homes they had viewed and asked them if they wanted to revisit any of them while they were still fresh in their mind.

Points to remember:
- *The Salesperson is a businessman looking for a return on his investment of time with a buyer.*
- *Be prepared and the salesperson won't waste your time.*
- *Decide on your Needs versus your wants.*

Chapter 7-The Salesperson seems "pushy!"

There is a saying that is one of the basic rules in the selling profession.

I call it the

"ABC of Selling"

ABC stands for "ALWAYS BE CLOSING"

More sales are lost by the Salesperson being too timid to ask for the order! It is a fact that Salespeople who don't succeed are the ones who are too scared of being rejected and won't ask for the order in case they get a 'no' from the customer. The experienced and successful Salespeople are the ones with a mindset that says we won't get a yes until we have had a few 'no's'. Here is a truism for you. The sale always starts with a no!

We won't go into that here but we will visit it a little later when we talk about buyer psychology and the psychology of the sale.

Would you be offended if, every time you said you liked something in a home, I blurted out "Want to buy the place?" It would be a bad move on my part and would quickly make you keep your comments to yourself, which is counterproductive to both sides.

I had a little technique that I called 'taking the buying temperature'. Lots of Salespeople use it and it is a very handy and non intrusive way of checking whether a buyer is interested in the home we are viewing.

Assume, if you will, that as you enter a home for the first time your 'buying temperature' is neutral. You neither like nor dislike the place. As we go through the home and you make a comment such as 'good sized lounge' I can take your buying temperature by asking you 'Is a large lounge important to you?' If you answer yes, you have just showed some enthusiasm for the home so your 'buying temperature' has risen. If your comment was adverse about the 'pokey kitchen' and I asked you about your comment, your 'buyer temperature' has gone down. Part of my job is to get your 'buying temperature' as high as possible so you want to buy the home.

Here is another insider truism.

If you don't like the home, there is no way on earth that we can make you buy the place. To call us Salespeople is really a misnomer and is a term that a lot of offices are trying to move away from by calling their Salespeople 'consultants' or 'advisers'.

A word of caution here.

There probably are a very small number of Salespeople in the industry who are more focussed on making the sale than assisting you make a desirable home buying decision. They generally don't last long in the business as their reputation gets around too quickly and they don't get any repeat or referral business. The biggest percentages of Salespeople are generally the ones who *wait for you to ask* to buy the home. That is why they don't make much of a living in Real Estate! The experienced and professional Salespeople have the expertise and confidence to make suggestions that may assist you in your buying decision. They will ask you what you don't like about a home and may come up with some ideas on the best way to address your concerns.

Experienced Salespeople see their role not as Salespeople who try to 'gouge' you into buying a home that you do not want. Our role is to assist you in making a purchasing decision. If you have a problem with one feature of the house but you love the rest of it, part of our role is to see if we can help you minimise your concern over the adverse feature.

One of the easiest ways to illustrate the value of using experienced Salespeople is to recall a buyer who absolutely loved the home we were viewing but would not commit to the purchase. Eventually I got out of her that she thought the lounge was just too dark. Without saying a word, I walked over to the windows and pulled back the net curtains to allow more light in. Her face glowed and she had signed her offer within the hour! It was such a simple thing to adjust that she could not see it. That is where you get the value from the experienced Salespeople. But you will only get that value if you are open with them.

What if you can't find a home you like?

Okay, you have seen 15 homes and not taken a shine to any of them. Usually that means you are looking outside of the correct price range and your expectations are too high for your budget. Using the car analogy again, you want to buy the 2012 Cadillac but you only want to pay the price for the 2005 Skoda! If you are in a cashed up position you could try going to the auction properties that appeal and hope for a desperate vendor with a low reserve price. If you are not in that position you may have to adjust your thinking a little. Lower your expectations or increase your budget.

Lower your expectations.

What about considering a suburb that is lower in prestige. We can't all afford to live in Manhattan or Chelsea and in a neighbouring suburb there may be just what you want for a lower price. There is a balancing relationship between quality of location or quantity of home. At least be open to looking in other suburbs

Increase your budget.

Either consider a longer mortgage term or increase your anticipated monthly mortgage payments. Either way, keep the communication open with your Salesperson as he may have the ideal home in his stock that he has not shown you because you were more adamant on your preferred location.

Move one step ahead now. You have seen the home you want. The experienced Salesperson will be aware that you are running hot. The rookie will be waiting for you to ask for the order. This is where sales psychology kicks in and this is where the Salesperson has to use some psychology to get your commitment

We are not too far away from discussing the 'closing techniques' that Salespeople use. Remember the comment about us being advisors rather than Salespeople and we will look at it again when we talk about 'closing the deal.'

Buyer habits and Buyer reluctance

If you have ever spent an hour or two looking for a new dress or a new suit, you may have looked at 20 choices. You see the one that you want. Great! You should state out loud that this is the suit you want. What happens? You dither! You may want to go and have another look at the one you saw in the other shop. This is generally a delaying tactic. As you are struggling to come to a decision *in case it is the wrong decision!*

This happens in maybe 80% of buyers. You buy food or newspapers with no hesitation every week and your buying habits are just that, HABITS!

When you come to make a decision on an infrequent purchase, you have no buying pattern to fall back on and most people get into a state of uncertainty *in case they make the wrong decision!*. Remember I said that this happens to 80% of purchasers when buying items that they buy infrequently. Think of your indecision the last time you purchased a car, shoes, wallpaper or carpets. Relatively expensive purchases that you will have for a relatively long time and you are uncertain in case you make the wrong decision. Believe me when I say it is natural to have that uncertainty.

The good Salesperson should be able to help you here. By asking you questions to polarise your thinking.

The first thing to reaffirm is your need or desires to make the purchase.

As an example, I always struggle with buying shoes. I always buy good quality slip on shoes that will last at least a year and don't mind paying a good price for the better quality product. I am unfamiliar with current trends and prices so when I enter the shoe shop I first have to accept the new price levels and then discover that my favourite style is no longer made. Last year when I was walking through a different town centre, I scuffed my shoe on a raised cobble and the sole of my right shoe just came away and folded back! I am about to go and give a talk to a sales team from another Office in another town. Without hesitation, I walked into the nearest shoe shop. I tried on two pairs of shoes and bought one pair. In and out of the shop in seven minutes with a new pair of shoes. I needed the shoes, choice was limited, and time was definitely limited. So what would normally have been an hour or more of wandering the shoe shops was condensed into seven minutes. No dithering, no indecision and I still have the shoes today. They are very comfortable.

There is a real parallel here to buying your new home. As Salespeople we probably give you too much choice and confuse you a little. Price is usually the last issue to be discussed. Does the home 'fit' you? Is it suitable for what you will be using it for (Lifestyle/storage etc) is it the right colour for you? You haven't seen anything else that jumps out at you and says, "Buy me! Buy me!". Answer those questions and you can probably buy your home.

There will never be a perfect home for you! If you had a home architecturally designed specifically to your needs, it would not be perfect. Within a year, your social habits or family/lifestyle habits will have changed and you are thinking of an extension or repapering the lounge to go with the new TV cabinet etc. If you are shown a home that fits you today better than anything else you have seen, you should consider buying it! Make some adjustments to your furniture. It may be just the right time to consider a new lounge suite or a new bedroom suite

We know you like the home

As I stated earlier, the Salesperson often knows before you do that you want to buy the home. *How?*

♦ Your body language (Moving your furniture in with hand gestures, Standing closer to your partner when you ask questions.)

- Your closer examination of certain rooms (master bedroom, kitchen and garage are the usual ones)
- Making sure the children are happy with their bedroom (so they won't object later when you buy the home)

The questions you ask are also different:....
- Will they leave the dishwasher?
- What are the rates on this place?
- What was the price again?
- What are the schools like here?

The Salesperson will 'ask for the order' in a fairly oblique manner to avoid forcing you to state that you do or do not want to purchase the home. He may state something like "From what you are saying, this home does seem to have all that you were looking for, doesn't it." It isn't a question as such. It is more a statement of fact that you can agree with or disagree.

For myself, at this point I did not want a clear yes! I wanted you to raise a concern that I could work on with you. I wanted you to say that it was okay but the prices is too high/ not enough garaging/ the gardens will take some looking after etc. If you raise a concern I can come back with something to the effect of "would you be interested in buying the home if we can address your concerns on the price/ garaging/ grounds etc.

This is all very basic salesmanship and is geared at helping you polarise your thinking. You have a simple decision to make.

If the price was $5,000 less would I buy it? Yes I would!

Big decisions and little decisions

Note that the decision you are now making is a relatively small one of price and not one of the huge decisions such as "Do I want to buy this house?" You have already moved past that stage in your mind. By asking the small question of price you have slipped past the big question of which house to buy. If you did not want this house you would not even consider the issue of price and would say so quickly. We have not tricked you, we have only helped to polarise your thinking to make your decision easier.

Compare it to buying the shoes. You have looked at twenty pairs of shoes. To make the decision easier you cut the choice down to two pairs and all the other shoes are taken away. The choice we are giving you is helping you cut your decision making down to just two choices. Buy or not buy.

The questions we asked you are what we call 'closing questions'. They are questions we ask to see if we can close the deal. Closing questions come in a wide range of subject (depending on the Salesperson) and a wide range of subtlety.

Here is the desired routine for the Salesperson.

a) Closing question
b) Buyer comes up with objection or states a concern.
c) Salesperson confirms that other than the main objection the buyer wants the home
d) Salesperson tries to address the objection or concern with suggestions.
e) Salesperson closes again

There is a mnemonic for the sequence that a lot of salesperson are taught and that mnemonic is

C.D.I.D.C.

Which stands for

C. Closing question, which should raise an objection or a concern
D. Dignify. Make the buyer comfortable that his concern is valid; (Use the 3 F's. Feel Felt, Found.)
I. Identify whether this is the real and main concern or a smokescreen and they don't want to buy this home.

D.   Disarm. Overcome the suggestion with a practical solution

C. Closing question again to confirm we have the buyer's true feelings about the home purchase.

A typical closing sequence may go like this

CLOSE. "From what you were looking for in your new home and what you have been saying about this property, do you feel this is the home you would like to move in to?"

Your reply. Well we like it but (for example) the lounge is way too dark for us.

DIGNIFY. "Well I understand how you *feel*. And other buyers have *felt* that way. I believe I have *found* a simple way to lighten up the lounge that will also make the next bedroom more warm as well."

IDENTIFY. "If I can address your concern on the lounge, would you consider making an offer to purchase this home?"

Your reply. Yes we would

DISARM. "Well if the willow tree was pruned or even removed from the garden it would lighten up the whole of this side of the home. It would be a lot warmer in winter as the sun would be coming in to the lounge nearly all day."

CLOSE.   **"How would it be if we made it a condition of the purchase that the vendor removes the tree prior to your moving in? We**

**could go back to the Office right now and write
that clause into your offer to purchase."**

Note that at no time have I asked you outright to
buy the home. Initially I asked would you like to
live here and in the second close I made the
suggestion that we put an extra clause in your offer
to purchase the home. At any point you can say
Whoa! All I have done is to polarise your thinking
to make the decision easier for you. If you don't
want the home you would have already made that
quite clear and the Salesperson would not be closing
the sale at this time or in this home.

If the above sounds like I am coercing you to buy
the home, the truth here is that if you had not shown
interest I probably would not have used a closing
question on you at all. And as we said above, there
are a number of ways that good Salespeople will see
you are interested. If I start closing on you and your
buying temperature is cold, I lose a lot of credibility
with you and I have to restart building your trust in
me.

As a buyer of anything you are constantly being
bombarded with "closing questions" that either
close the sale or enhance the sale. If you go to buy a
car, the close may be along the lines of "If you were
to buy this car, would you prefer a 24 month or a 36
month payment plan?". You may end up deciding
on the term of finance rather than the big decision
of "Do you want to buy this car?" if you don't think

you would fall for lines like the one above, how many times have you responded to the sales enhancement line?

The best sales enhancement close of all time? It increased turnover by around $120 Million a year in Britain alone! The close is so simple.

"And would you like Fries with that?"

At least you now know what to listen for!

Points to remember:
- *Big decisions and little decisions.*
- *You are here to buy a house, we are here to sell you a house. Don't get defensive if the Salesperson tries to sell you something. It's why you are here, isn't it?*
- *Salespeople are trained to **help you** buy.*
- *They know you want to buy, often before you do!*

Chapter 8 - Sales Psyche

You are probably sat at home right now, reading this book, so it would not be taking you out of your comfort area if we digress for a few pages and talk about some of the psychology of selling and buying and also some of the basic training techniques that a new salesperson goes through and uses on you with greatly varying degrees of skill and subtlety.

Let's talk briefly about how the buyer's mindset changes when they find something they really like.

The buyer's desires are, most of the time, centred on the need to satisfy one or more of the following areas:-

- Profit.
- Pride.
- Position.
- Growth.
- Retirement.
- Family

All are pretty self-explanatory so there is no need to delve further. Before you make your move, identify to yourself which of, or how many of, the six basic needs above are your reason for moving and always keep that fact in mind when you are talking to your Salesperson

The Buying Mindset / Progression of desire

Now we move on to the progression of your buying enthusiasm.

In *nearly all* buying situations the progression of the buyer's mindset goes something very like this

Desire -- Need -- Want -- Want real bad -- Fear of loss

You will never buy anything until you have first established a …

DESIRE. Even if it just a casual remark such as "This place is too small, we really would be more comfortable in a four bed home". The desire, however trivial or serious has been established. The seed has been planted in your brain and your brain, being the magnificent machine that it is, works quietly in the background and you suddenly start to find yourself glancing at the Real Estate pages in the newspaper.

NEED is a growth of the desire. You have seen a few homes in the paper that you 'wouldn't mind having a look at'. Your initial casual comment has now taken you on a course of action. Your brain is now telling you that you need the bigger home or at least you need to look at bigger homes.

WANT comes out into the open when you see something that you quite like. Maybe it is more than you think you can afford but your thought processes are now sufficiently turned on to perhaps approach the bank to see if you can borrow a few more dollars.

WANT REAL BAD! The bank says you can borrow a few more dollars. Not quite enough to buy the home you have set your mind on and that makes you want it even more! (Call it human nature!) The pivotal factor here may not be the bank; it may be that you have to sell your home first or whatever. There is usually a negative or delaying factor that changes your buying temperature from 'Want' to 'Want real bad!'

FEAR OF LOSS. This is the danger zone. Not everybody reaches this stage. Often the Salesperson may feed your 'Want real bad' temperature with a little fuel to raise your buying temperature up to "fear of loss" level. This is the stage where you make decisions that are often hurried and without full forethought. A little panic steps in. The Salesperson may feed you the line that there are other buyers waiting to view this home and it seems like this would be the perfect home for them etc. If you don't make an offer to purchase you may lose out. The 'fear of loss' often makes you jump in. Like I said earlier, this is the danger zone. You really need to have a top Salesperson on your side that can advise you honestly. Is there really another buyer waiting? Often buyers make an offer subject to the sale of their own home. What happens if you don't get the sale price you wanted for your own place?

Some words of caution

From personal experience. A Real Estate Salesperson showed me a luxury block of 4 flats for me to purchase at $260,000 in 1990. I was assured I would get $250,000 for my home. So I entered into a deal. I bought the flats for $255,000 and $180,000 was left in as vendor finance for 12 months while I sold my home. By listening to the Salesperson I was well and truly stitched up. The flats were worth no more than $210,000. I eventually sold my home, 15 months later, for $180,000. The vendor was on my back for his money and threatening to put me in bankruptcy. The only thing that saved me from bankruptcy was my solicitor who suggested that as I had lost everything other than the shirt on my back, I had nothing to lose. I should tell the vendor that he could put me into bankruptcy and he would get nothing or he could take the flats back and let me get on with my life. He eventually took the latter option but it cost me over $15,000 in legal fees and

I had lost everything I had worked for because I had listened to a fat and lazy Real Estate Salesperson who was only interested in his commission. It was a very expensive lesson for me and it was one of the factors that made me go into Real Estate. I could not have been any worse than the Salesperson that advised me and I could probably do a whole lot better. My weakness or vulnerability and subsequent losses came from going into the 'fear of loss' zone and believing and acting on the Salesperson's advice in his estimations of what I could get for my home.

Consumer legislation today means that I could have sued the Salesperson or the Agent for everything if I could have withstood the extra strain. But in the end, we just got on with our lives and I became the best Real Estate Salesperson that I could be and spent time and effort developing a reputation for honest dealing.

As I became more successful I realised that the commission dollars were not the goal in my dealings. If I did my job well I sold houses and the money came in anyway. So my end goal was always focused on the selling results rather than the dollar results.

Another mnemonic that we were taught in basic training that stayed with me right through my career was

C.R.E.A.T.E.

C.R.E.A.T.E trains the Salesperson to try and generate or feed the 'fear of loss' mindset. It goes like this. I've written the text from a salespersons point of view. Try to get into their mindset when you read it.

- **CREATE**. Create confidence. Make the buyer or seller like you. Try and find some mutual ground or friends. Praise them for something that they have or something they have done. Make them see you as Mr Nice Guy rather than a Real Estate Salesperson. When it comes down to picking between two or three Salespeople, if most other things are equal, a buyer will go with the guy they feel most comfortable with.

- **REVITALISE.** When you sense you have their trust, revitalise their mind that you are here to talk business. By revitalising the vendor's mind you get them into the state of being enthusiastic about you selling their home.

- **EVINCE.** Evince logically. Evince is just another word for talking. Use logics in your patter only briefly. Only one in twenty people want to know that the average sale in the area for the last 5.1 months was at 12.223% over the G.V, which is an increase of 2.19% over the preceding 3.4 months. A little logic and statistics is okay but you stand a good chance of becoming the Real Estate professor rather than the Real Estate friend if you use too much logic

- **AROUSE.** Arouse desire for them to work with you and your company. You are the biggest/best/ most fun to work with etc, Find out what they want through 'Venting' (I'll tell you later) and feed that back to them

- **TRIGGER**. Trigger urgency. This is where we step into the realm of promoting the 'fear of loss'. "If you sign the listing today we will get you into the 'property magazine'. There are only three spots left and they are being grabbed quickly, However the Boss wants to be fair and he said that the first three Salespeople in with the signed listing form will get the spots. So if you sign now I will shoot back to the office and do my best to make sure that one of the spots features your home." Smooth? Possibly or probably true but the 'fear of loss' is right up in front in this patter.

- **EFFECT**. Effect a close. Ask the question. Don't say "will you sign the listing form, please?' That is a big decision. Try an oblique close. "Once you have signed the listing, I was thinking of putting the For Sale sign over by the tree or would you prefer it closer to the gate?

In variations of the above, that is a basic patter that many Salespeople will use. The better Salesperson doesn't need to use it as much because most of their listings and buyers come from referrals. With a referral client the Salesperson needs to spend less time selling himself and gets on to the other tasks sooner. In my last four months of selling homes, I signed up twenty new listings. Seventeen of the twenty were from repeat clients or referred clients. The other three just walked into my open homes. As I was going into a management position with an opposition group I was, quite rightly, not prospecting for new listings. But they just kept coming to me, which is, I suppose a testament to my local standing and the high service standards I was known for.

Let's take a quick look at how Salespeople learn their little phrases and patter lines and then we can possibly see why so few of them take the next step to become a part of the elite level.

When you, or anybody, is given new lines to learn, the learning and accepting process goes through four stages before you can forget the learning process and the lines become automatic to you.

For the example below, think back to your school days when you first learned the alphabet. Remember back that far? Now I know you can remember your alphabet now. I bet you can even remember that little tune they used to get you to remember and learn all the letters. Right?

There is a set pattern to learning and accepting new lines such as the alphabet or the national anthem and it happens over 4 separate stages.

OK. The four stages of learning or accepting new lines of sales patter (or your alphabet) into your psyche are these:-

- Phoney.
- Uncomfortable.
- Comfortable.
- Habit.

- *Phoney.* The lines are not in your usual vocabulary. They are not phrases you would use or the vocal inflections are different. They feel and sound phoney to you. You are told to go and practise them in front of a mirror five times a day for seven days.

- **Uncomfortable.** Ok, so now you can spit out the lines without stumbling over them but you still feel they are not part of you. Go and practise them some more, please.

- **Comfortable.** So the practising paid off. Now you can just trot them out and they are part of your vocabulary and phrasing. When the need arises, you would be able to repeat them with no problem. Keep the practice up.

- **Habit.** This is the stage where only the good performers get to. When they are making a close on the sale they do not have to remember which line to bring out in response to your last reply. The line or its variation will come out automatically. The benefit of achieving this level of mastery of your patter is this. A Salesperson that has only reached the 'comfortable' stage of mastering his lines has to stop momentarily, after receiving your response to his close, in order to work out which line he should be using next. So while he is listening to you, he is only half listening as his thoughts are also calculating his correct response. The top Salesperson that has reached the 'habit' stage is focussed totally on your response and can react automatically to you. That level of expertise only comes from practice, practice and more practice.

Try this question now; what is the next letter in the alphabet after the letter 'F'. The answer is, of course, 'G'. Did you have to go through the alphabet or did you know it automatically? Automatically right? You are at the 'habit stage' through your practice all those years ago and you can still trot it out now some 20, 30 or 40 years later without thinking. If you had not practised them years ago you would not be able to trot them out today. Your teacher and your parents made you practise them!

Salespeople today, and this is a very sweeping generalisation, have so much to learn and have so much pressure on them to perform on day one that they have to learn and master some things and let other things slide and hope to get back to them in the future some time. Conversely, in the 'Bums on Seats' mentality that offices had in the 90's they would take just about any one on and hope they survived. The extremely high attrition rate of up to 95% in the first 2 years is testimony to either the toughness of the job or the general unsuitability of the people that Agents were taking in as Salespeople to satisfy the 'Bums on Seats' mentality.

Either way, the 'average' Salesperson in the Real Estate industry is not a high performing or high earning individual. There is a saying that the Real Estate industry falls into the 80/20 rules. That means that only 20% of the Salespeople earn 80% of all the commission! I personally feel that the figure is more like 70/30. But it still means that 20% or 30% of Salespeople are earning 70% or 80% of all the commission. For you, this means you have only a 1 in 4 chance of teaming up with a capable and competent career Salesperson who will have your best interests at heart and be fully capable of advising you in the disposal and acquisition of your property needs. That is a pretty scary thought folks!

If I were allowed to make just one point in the whole of this book, it would be this.

Never ever just walk into a Real Estate Office and accept the duty Salesperson as your Salesperson. From experience, every Salesperson has to take a part on the duty roster, and that means always having a Salesperson available in the office for casual 'walk in' business. The busier (usually that means better) Salesperson is too busy working with clients and has asked a junior Salesperson to take on their duty time.

To increase your chances of getting the good Salesperson, ask around at work for a Salesperson that one of your colleagues or friends will recommend. Ask them why they recommend that particular Salesperson.

If you are moving to a new town and have no friends in that town, phone up all the Real Estate Offices and ask the receptionist for the name of their top Salesperson and ask to speak to that person. Ring five or six offices to ensure that you get a good selection of top Salespeople.

A few pages back I used the term "venting" and said I would explain it later. Now is a good time.
Ever had a Salesperson in your home that spent quite some time explaining how he was the best Salesperson? Won all the awards etc, his office was the biggest, brightest and best, his office advertised most, made most sales, had the biggest referral network etc?

As a Salesperson I knew that every other Salesperson would be trying to convince the potential client of their worth as an individual salesperson etc and I could not be bothered competing if that was all I had to match. We cannot all be the biggest/brightest /best etc so some of them had to be telling porkies and I believe it got a little confusing and boring for the clients. I had a different technique, which I called 'venting'. It was not my original idea as I heard somebody talking about it and I just developed it for my personal style.

While talking to a potential vendor I would ask them the question, "when you have dealt with other Salespeople in selling or buying your homes, may I ask what you found positive in that Salesperson or what annoyed you most?" As the client told me that the biggest complaint about the other Salesperson was – never heard from him/ did not do open homes/did not put up a sign/ no market feedback/ assistants did the open homes etc. They were giving me my script for when I went to market myself to them later. I could now tell them what they wanted to hear. My presentation included the facts that I – contacted them every week/ commit to at least one open home every week and more if they would allow me/ the sign went up within 10 minutes of the listing being signed/I contacted them after every client had been through the home/I never allowed anyone other than myself to do the open homes as I was the expert on their home etc. It was much more relevant to the client than a whole list of my achievements (real or pretend)

In closing this chapter, I always recall one of my training mentors words to me when I asked her why so many people fail to succeed in our industry. Her reply was:

" Humans are creatures of predictable buying habits. The good Salesperson is trained to identify them and help them with their purchases. The poor salesperson is too scared of being thought pushy and is too busy trying to be their frien d."

It's something that has always stuck with me. If a salesperson is considered pushy, it might be clumsiness on their part, but at least they are doing their job!

Back to business. You have found a home you might like to live in! Great stuff!\

Points to remember:
- *Always remember why you are buying a new home.*
- *Avoid going into the 'fear of loss' mindset.*

Chapter 9- you have found the house to buy!

What is the next step?

Generally the Salesperson or his office will initially prepare the agreement. Often, the solicitor will also be involved. To be binding, the offer to purchase must be in writing. A verbal agreement is not worth the paper it is written on (to quote Samuel Goldwin) and I would never advise a client to consider a verbal offer.

The Salesperson and you confer on the details that will make up your offer - settlement date/ price/deposit/ confirm chattels/ confirm extra conditions you want included etc etc. Let's go over some of your considerations at this time and look at the information you will want to ensure goes into your offer to purchase

Contract considerations
- ***Purchasers.***

Yourself? Or you and your partner? A family trust? Are all signatory's of legal age to sign the agreement or are guardians necessary?
- ***Legal description.***

What is the correct legal estate of the property? Freehold, cross lease. Unit title? Ask your Salesperson to explain the differences and the pitfalls of unit title and cross lease titles. Are there any easements or right of ways over the land? What is the section size? Is there a copy of the title available for you to look at? How long do people stay as owners of this property on average? (Regular changes could indicate a problem in the neighbourhood)

- *Deposit.*

There is no legal requirement for you to pay 10% deposit on signing. The Salesperson will be asking you for at least 6% (so he can get paid sooner). If both parties agree to having a nil deposit, that is quite acceptable and binding for the agreement. However, putting down a significant deposit does indicate to the vendor that you are a serious and substantial buyer and your offer is to be taken seriously. However, you don't need to pay the deposit until the agreement is unconditional provided that you state that in your offer to purchase. The deposit is held by the Real Estate Agent in his Trust account as the neutral stakeholder between the parties.

- *L.I.M report.*

If you are new to the district, you should consider seeing a LIM report on the property. L.I.M stands for Land Information Memorandum. It may be called by a different name in your locality. It is a report on the property and the area and the zoning, which is prepared by the local council or territorial authority and will give you some information to consider before the Agreement becomes unconditional.

- *Settlement date.*

Work out the dates so that there are at least two weeks that elapse between the settlement date and fulfilment dates for any extra conditions you want to insert into the agreement. Unconditional date and settlement date should never be the same day and a two-week separation of those dates would be a minimum unless there are other circumstances to consider. Where necessary, if you are selling your home and moving into the new place on the same day, make sure those days are matched in your offer to purchase

- *Finance clause.*

The most common condition in agreements is the clause that states this agreement is conditional on the purchaser arranging finance to complete the purchase. For your own protection, fill in the clause accurately. Insert the finance institution you will approach, the amount you wish to borrow and the amount of time you need to make the application. It is too complicated to go into here, but the more accurate the detail you insert here, the greater your protection should you need to pull out of the deal.

- *Chattels.*

Probably the major source of arguments and ill feelings at the settlement time. There will be a list of chattels that you are aware of that stay with the property at the time of sale. Chattels usually include Stove, carpets, blinds, drapes, TV aerial and phone. Those are listed on the agreement on the front page. Make sure that everything you believe stays with the property is on the agreement you sign. I once

had a vendor who insisted on taking the washing machine taps with her, as they were not on the chattels list. Someone had to suddenly come up with $200 to replace the taps and as usual the Salesperson is the first one they look at. It cost me the $200, as I wanted the buyer to be happy with what I had done rather than be angry at the actions of the vendor. I even went round and fitted the new taps in myself the following day. Because of my gesture, the buyer understood it was not my fault and met me halfway and gave me $100 back. Confession time here. The vendor also felt a little guilty afterwards and also gave me $100. Both clients used me again for their future Real Estate needs and I still came out as Mr Nice Guy because of the way I handled the situation. As I said on the opening page of this book it is not too hard to shine in this industry if you apply yourself a little and put yourself out a little.
\

Arguments over chattels often come down to the definitions of chattels and fixtures and fittings. Carpets and rugs are a good example. If a carpet is fitted and 'nailed down' it is regarded as a fixture as opposed to a rug which is not fitted. In determining the definitions, the courts assess the 'degree of annexation' actual and intended. That is way too complicated. Put it in if you want it and if you know something is excluded, make a note of that also.

- *Special Conditions page*.

Here is where you put in all the conditions you want included in the agreement. If you want a valuation or inspection by a builder put it in here. You want your solicitor to check things out or you want to check out the building files etc, it goes in here. You may not know what you want or need so the Salesperson should be advising you all the time. If you have any doubt check it out with your solicitor. Once the agreement is signed it is binding on both parties. Having said that, a good solicitor can get you out of most agreements if there are some things he can work on. As a guide, always put in the clause that the agreement is subject to your solicitor's approval.

Any extra conditions you put in here have to be agreed to by the vendor. It happens occasionally that the vendor, as part of his counteroffer, may also include a condition or two, which you may have to consider.

The more conditions that go into an offer means that there are more opportunities for the deal to fall over and that means it becomes less acceptable to the vendor. It is something to think about, especially if you are starting with a cheeky offer to test the vendor's motivation. Later on in the book we will be talking about negotiating and negotiating tactics so I won't go into that here other than repeating the advice we gave about how to counter offer.

The key thing here is to go in with an offer that will tempt the vendor. So let's see what we can do to get the vendor excited.

Make the most of your offer

You want the house. And you are quite keen to buy it. You have resisted the urge to go into the 'fear of loss' mindset despite the Salesperson's best efforts. You know the vendor wants to be moved within 6 weeks and that fits in with your schedule as well.
Things are looking good!
The home is on the market at $210,000 and you figure you will pay no more than $200,000. You decide that your opening offer is going to be $190,000. The only condition is that of you arranging the mortgage.

What is the biggest fear you have?

If you don't have a fear, the Salesperson should be advising you that you stand the risk of offending the vendor with an offer that is too low. What can then happen is that the vendor's ego can get in the way and although he may have settled for $200,000, he is offended and now won't take less than $205,000. If you really want the home you may have just spent, or at least risked, an extra $5,000 through being too cheeky! If your top dollar is $200,000 why not go in with your first offer at $195,000. In the old days of negotiating, both sides seem to have a mindset that we go in low and meet in the middle. In this example, we will agree on $200,000 as the price. Fortunately the Salespeople are better trained at negotiating and we try to discourage that old mindset of meeting in the middle.

Go back and look at how to counter offer and we will talk of the negotiating tricks later.

> *Points to remember:*
> - *Prepare the agreement so it reflects what **you** want to say.*
> - *If in doubt, see your solicitor.*
> - *Make the offer as attractive as you can.*

Chapter 10 –How good is your Salesperson?

For now we will take a few pages on some of the ways you can check out how effective your Salesperson is while he is acting on your behalf. And also cover some of the tips and tricks to get the best from your Salesperson.

Advertising

Every year the average Real Estate Office spends around $100,000 on their advertising. Some offices may spend 2, 3 or even 10 times that amount and some will only spend $25,000. The amount they spend is governed by the amount the other companies in the area spend. On the perception the public hold that "bigger is better", if one Office has a full page advert, the other offices have to have a full page advert or the public perceives them as being smaller in size and effectiveness. If one Office starts to advertise using colour ads, you can almost bet that within twelve months, most of the competition will be in colour as well.

In our town, the cost of colour adverts is an extra $325 per week. For a brief period the first company into colour will enjoy an advantage. By the end of the year when every company is into colour, nobody has the advantage other than the local newspaper that now take in an extra $325 per week times ten Offices times fifty two weeks. That adds up to a quite significant extra $169,000 for the newspaper in increased revenue. That is now another $169,000 that the Offices have to find out of their commission income. Often the move into colour or the increase in advert size is taken in order to keep their sales team happy and to prevent them from moving over to another company that has gone into colour advertising or something similar.

Whatever an Office spends in advertising, they spend it for just three main reasons.

- The first reason is because the other companies advertise! A company at a nearby large town tried to not advertise in the Newspaper for 4 weeks as an experiment. The nett result was that the phone rang 3 times as often! With advertising today, most buyers read the paper and go along to the Open home without contacting the office or the salesperson. So there is no phone call. With this experiment people had to ring the office for information and business actually increased!

- The second reason is to keep the team happy. If the opposition is advertising two full pages a week in the newspapers, the Salespeople want the same level in case the public think the other office is bigger / brighter / better! Remember that we have said a number of times earlier that perception is reality and the public do buy into the 'bigger adverts equate to a bigger/better company".

- The third reason is to make the phone ring! The Office can even do a calculation on how much each phone call costs by monitoring for a month the amount of times a phone rings and dividing that amount by the cost of that months advertising. Some months, the cost of each phone enquiry can be well in excess of $100 per call.

-

I am getting to the point now of the explanation.

If the phone goes after hours and the call goes to the Salesperson's home, often the call is wasted. Most of the calls concerning the advert the Office has paid for your home's profile will be taken at the Salesperson's home rather than at his Office. Check out for yourself how good your Salesperson is when you have read the next few paragraphs.

Imagine you have read the advert for your property and want more info. To get to this point you have trawled your way through ten or twenty pages of adverts and have circled five or six homes that you want more info about. Your mindset is that of deleting the home from your shopping list. You have already skipped through 10,000 homes and narrowed your selection down to the five or six you have circled.

When you ring up for the info, you will delete it quickly if it does not meet your most pressing criteria. Trust me on this one! It is correct. The advert says 3 bedrooms in sought after area and the price of $159,000 is in your range. You ring up the afterhour's number and the phone is answered by a teenager who has not been taught how to answer the phone politely. You ask for the Salesperson and the teenager shouts out, "Dad, it's for you!" It would have been nice if he had moved the phone away from his mouth before he shouted for dad. Dad comes to the phone and is reasonably cheerful and polite. You ask about the property, does it have a double garage? The answer is no, so you say thank you and put the phone down. Remember earlier we said that the one enquiry could cost the company over $100? The Salesperson has just wasted $100. The above was a scenario for an average Salesperson that is repeated hundreds of times every day in every part of the country. If you don't believe me, take the test!

The good Salesperson will handle the enquiry differently. His kids will have been taught to answer the phone politely. When you ask for the Salesperson they will ask you to hold, while they get him to the phone. The Salesperson in response to your enquiry for the double garage will take control of the conversation by saying something to the effect that "No, it does not have a double garage, were you looking for a home with a double garage?" You answer 'yes'. He continues, "May I ask you, that particular home is in the Glenford area, were you looking for that area specifically?" You answer that you are open to the area as long as it is not too rough and it has a double garage. He responds, "The price in the advert was $159,000. Is that what you were looking to spend or do you have a higher budget?" You reply that you wanted to spend no more than $167,500. He then says that he has another five possible properties that he can show them to you?"

Which of the 2 salespeople is the more effective?

If you were paying for the advert for your property, which Salesperson would you want to answer the phone? It's fairly easy to check out how they answer the phone isn't it? Over to you!

Out of town referrals.

The good Salesperson will offer to forward your name to another Office in your new location if you are moving out of town, He will arrange for a Salesperson from that other town to give you a ring and perhaps forward some local listings for you to peruse. He will ensure that you get the top Salesperson from that office to contact you as he gets a referral commission from any home that you buy.

The poor Salesperson will recommend that you contact their local office when you get there. Some of the better and busier Salespeople can make up to an extra $10,000 a year by referral commissions. All for the sake of a few phone calls or faxes or emails.

How much does the average salesperson earn?

How much does the average Salesperson earn in your town? This will not work in large centres as the statistics overlap and Salespeople work in more than one area. However, if you live in a town rather than a metropolis, try this exercise.

You will need a calculator. 3 or 4 times a year, your local newspaper will give out the bad news that Real Estate is in a slump or even that it is on the rise. At that time, they give out the number of sales per year or per month and the average sale price reached. Tear the article out of the paper and put it to one side. Now go through the newspaper and count how many residential Salespeople are currently working in your town. Get this figure reasonably accurate. Here is where you need the calculator. Multiply the average sale price in your town by 4%. That will give you an average amount of commission earned per sale. Multiply that commission by the number of sales, which will give you the amount of commission earned across all Salespeople. Divide that amount by the number of Salespeople which indicates how much gross commission on average each Salesperson earned for the office and divide that amount by 50% which will give an indication of how much the average Salesperson will earn in your town in average month or year. If you thought they were earning an average of $100,000 each you will be shocked at what they earn for the amount of hours and effort that they put in. If you apply the 70/30 rule, you will not be surprised that the income level does not attract the top quality people into the industry.

Most of the top people in Real Estate have been doing it for a long time. In Real Estate that means five years or more. Occasionally you get the bright spark that comes in and makes mega dollars for the first two or three years and then burns out and leaves.

In Australia, one state (Queensland I believe) has a law that all Real Estate Salespeople have to receive a minimum wage, which is set at something like $400 per week. However the Offices over there do make you earn it. A Salesperson is fined $20 for every open home less than ten open homes. Another $10 comes off for every $100 under the budget of vendor advert contributions brought in. A Salesperson must have so many price reductions or more money is lost.

The Author gets on his soapbox for a couple of pages!

As a personal belief that will not take off in many countries, I feel we are looking at the whole set up of Real Estate marketing from the wrong viewpoint.

If you compare us to the sex industry there are a number of similarities.

- We will both do almost anything to get the dollars from clients who want our specialised service.
- Neither of us enjoy a high social status
- We can get into our respective industries with relatively little training.
- The ones who take extra training or provide extra good service will generally get more dollars

- The best operators make very good money
- We both put up with a considerable amount of 'moaning' from our clients (sic)

The main difference between us and the sex industry is that they get their money up front and they get paid regardless of the satisfaction or results achieved. Oh, and we put up with a sight more than thirty minutes of clients moans!

I believe that by operating as we do, working for nothing unless we achieve a successful sale, we have put ourselves in a position to be abused.

There is little incentive for the average Salesperson to better themselves educationally or to undertake up skilling programmes unless they make the decision to stay in the industry for the long term. The exams that I took to obtain my higher industry qualifications probably cost me around $30,000 in course and exam fees and the study time which took me away from being available to work with clients and earn an income.

I have written and sold a CD-Rom specifically targeted at the Real Estate Offices with several ideas that will change the way their teams do business. Ultimately they will make a whole lot more money and probably charge vendors less! The unfortunate thing is that a number of offices have to go with the ideas, as one office on their own will not be strong enough to make the change.

The most radical idea would be to change the way clients are charged. Instead of charging say $9,000 for the successful sale of your $200,000 home. How would you as a vendor feel if there was a way you would only pay maybe half that amount? Would you be willing to look at that system?

The simple idea is that the vendor pays a monthly fee of $1500 for a set time of 3 months, which covers all the marketing costs. There is no extra to pay for a successful sale. In effect you are renting the Salesperson and his experience and marketing expertise for the three months period.

Radical? Definitely!

Workable? Definitely!

The monthly fee would vary from area to area but would be set at 50% to 60% of the average commission for an area.

The biggest advantage to the vendors would be that they could ask whatever price they wanted for the property with the Salesperson's advice on the market levels. The Salesperson would not be always trying to crunch the vendor on price so he could make a sale and put food on his table.

The downside to the vendor is that he would have to be aware that the decisions he makes relative to the marketing of his home are now at his own cost. It would not take long for the best Salespeople to become apparent and build a reputation. The vendors may even be willing to pay a premium for the top Salespeople. Just as you would for a top solicitor or doctor or plumber or mechanic.

As I said earlier, it is radical for Real Estate

As I sit here in my office writing this book, I take a look around my bookshelf. There at least 150 books on my shelves, books on Law, Accounting, Personal Leadership, Computing, Motivation, Marketing and Management techniques.
There are a further 50 or more audiotapes on the same or similar subjects. There are also notes from the, perhaps, 100 or more training and education seminars I have attended over the last 15 years.

All these have been purchased by myself in an ongoing effort to be among the best prepared and knowledgeable Salesperson or Agent in town. I am no different from the other better performing Salespeople that invest time and money in themselves every year to keep abreast of developments. Having said all that I have some difficulty in accepting that my expertise is worthy of less respect than the mechanic or plumber etc who you will willingly pay for without a second thought.

As I said at the beginning of this portion, the author is getting on his soapbox.

Would you be interested in a scheme like the above?

Just in closing on this subject, let's go through a scenario.

If you needed to urgently quit your $200,000 home *today*, what price would you have to ask that would guarantee a sale *today*?

Work with me, please, on this one.

It would sell for $1 wouldn't it! At $1,000 it is a goner as well. At $50,000 it should be gone by lunchtime. At $100,000 it should still be gone today. If you said you would accept $130,000 you may have to wait a day? If you said $150,000 it may take a couple of days. How long would it take to sell at $175,000? A week? We know that it will take on average, in your area, 60 days to sell if you were looking for $190,000 to $200,000. If you wanted $225,000 we already know it will probably take 6 to 12 months or more.

You have just gone through the price/time equation. The more you want or will accept, the longer it will take to sell. Do you accept that as a fact?

You should!

Think of this also, the decision you make on the price you want to offer your home to the market for, has probably the biggest bearing on the time your home will be on the market. That is a logical progression from the previous paragraph.

So the next thought you should have is the realisation that you as the vendor, by dictating the price your home is presented to the market at, have the most control over the length of time you stay on the market!!!!!!!

Be the market good or bad you must accept that the market state will have some bearing on the *Fair market value* of your home. If the market is buoyant and there is a shortage of homes in your price range, your home increases in its market value or the time frame for selling your home reduces. It is a simple matter of supply and demand. Conversely, if the market is down or there is an oversupply of homes for sale in your price range you will have to reduce your price or wait a lot longer for the sale. Again, is it is simply a matter of supply and demand.

In most situations, the vendor is in control of the time factor due to the vendor's stipulation of his asking price. Does that sound logical to you? It should do! With the above-mentioned scenario of hiring the Salesperson, the vendor chooses the speed of the sale without jeopardising the

Salespersons income and the vendor saves himself perhaps half of the commission bill!

As I said earlier, it is radical but a very common sense way of selling your home at a reasonable cost. Let's move on and dispel a few myths that we come across often in our work as a Real Estate Salesperson.

We have already shown you how to work out what the average Salesperson earns in your area.

Here is another common cry we hear from vendors. " We are moving to ABC (A major city) from XYZ (A small rural town) so we want more for our home." Firstly, if the situation was reversed and you were moving to XYZ from ABC, would you be selling your home for 50% less than the market would want to pay? That answer is a resounding 'NO'. So why should the reverse happen because you are moving to a dearer location? Secondly, as we have discussed several times in this book, the only factors to consider in assessing the 'Fair market value' of your home are the state of the market and how your home measures up to its competition and the urgency of the sale. Included in how your home measures up to its competition are all the variables that include location, size, style, and amenities.

Points to remember:
How hard is it to find a good Salesperson?
To Paraphrase George Orwell-
"All Salespeople are created equal, but some Salespeople are more equal than others"

Chapter 11 - How do you find out the level of your competition and assess a likely time on the market?

Conversely, if you are a buyer, would it be handy for you to know how much competition there is in the price range you want to purchase in? Would it help you in your negotiating?

It's worth trying the following

You only need to know two factors.

Let's assume your home is worth $200,000 on today's market. You need to know how many homes are on the market today in the price range of, say, $190,000 to $215,000. That is easy to find. Get the local property paper or newspaper and count the number of homes for sale in that price range from the adverts. As a precaution, add another 10% to your count, as not every home is advertised every time. Even easier, go to the local Real estate website for your area that has multiple companies subscribing to it. Do a search for all homes in your approximate price range. Then do the sums.

The other factor you need to know is the number of homes that have sold in that price range in the last four to six months. When you have that information, divide it back to an average monthly figure. Ask your Salesperson to supply that information from his statistical information. If he is a good Salesperson he will supply you with a copy of that information so you can check the sales are appropriate.

Let's work on a couple of scenarios.

Case 1. There are an average of six sales per month in your price range and there are fourteen other properties on the market. That's fifteen properties including yours. Divide fifteen properties by six sales per month and the average sale in your price range is taking 2.5 months. Also be aware, from the above figures that there is 2.5 months supply of stock in your price range. That is a pretty reasonable supply/ demand figure. Given that your home stands well among its competition, you could reasonably expect to be sold within two to three months.

Case 2. There are an average of six sales per month in the price range but there are another sixty-five properties in competition with your home. Sixty-six properties divided by six sales per month means that there is eleven months stock available on the market in your price range. That presents a massive oversupply for only six sales per month. Can you see you may have a problem? A problem that need your urgent consideration if you want to sell in less than eleven months?

You have a few options to consider.

Firstly bring your price down to make it attractive. However, a drop of $2,000 will have little or no impact with that much competition, you may have to consider a drop of $10,000 to really make your home appealing and put it into the next lower price range as a good buy. Another option is to fund a high impact advertising campaign to lift your profile above its competition. The third option is to be prepared to sit and wait for the market to take a shift in its supply / demand ratio. The fourth option is the one that too few people think of. Take your home off the market for six to twelve months until the market picks up. If you don't have a pressing need to sell today, a better option may be to wait. You possibly may not have to drop your price as much or you may save having to pay out $2,000 or more for an advertising campaign that may or may not work.

"I will hold out for my price as I want to buy a dearer home and I need as much as I can get for this home."

This is another common cry Real Estate Salespeople hear and they have to be very logical in their explanations to overcome this comment. Salespeople have discovered already that a home is only worth what a buyer will pay for it! (We have taken that point on board haven't we?) The only way to get more for the home is to either add value (install a dishwasher / extra room/ new carpets etc) or wait for the property values around you to rise.

The first option involves an investment of dollars. When you add $10,000 of new carpets, it will not increase the value by the amount you have invested. The same goes for almost all other cosmetic inputs. It may speed up the sale but you will lose money taking that option. The second option involves an investment of time. As a scenario you need 10% more for your $200,000 home so you can afford to buy a $300,000 home. If you get $220,000 You have an $80,000 gap to bridge. After a year, your home has risen in value by 10% and you get your $220,000. Unfortunately the $300,000 home has also risen in value by 10% and will now cost you $330,000. By waiting for your price, the gap to bridge has now risen from $80,000 to $110,000! Sometimes you just can't win! The key to resolving this dilemma is to be realistic about what your home is worth today and strive to get that amount for it and make your next purchase fit the reality of the market and your budget!

"But I have spent so much in extras on the home it has to be worth at least $30,000 more than anything else on the market."

In your neighbourhood or town, there has to be an area that is generally regarded as a pretty rough area. Mainly flats and state housing etc. The average price of the homes in this area is maybe $70,000 in a town that has an average value of $160,000. Okay, you have the place in mind? Right, now imagine if you were to fit out a home in that area with a new spa pool, a new swimming pool, double garage with auto doors, a new Italian kitchen and new carpets throughout. You have just spent a little under $60,000 on the place and it is looking like a dream. It is now time to put it on the market. Average value in the area is $70,000 plus the $60000 you have spent would mean an asking price of $130,000 wouldn't it? Would you get it? Would you get $100,000? $90,000? $85,000 surely! You would be giving it away at $82,500 wouldn't you? What do you think you would get for it? Remember it is the worst area in town.

The sad fact is that so many people overcapitalise on their home and they will never recoup their investment. Location is a key factor in the pricing of a home and is as important as the market condition in assessing 'fair market value'. The ideal place to sell is the worst home in the best street. It is a Salesperson's dream. The best home in the worst street is the Salesperson's nightmare. As a last thought on this subject, I was once asked to appraise a home for a Dutch chap. He was a nice guy but very straight talking. He had built the home himself ten years prior and it was magnificently built and laid out. He wanted around $18,000 more than I and a colleague appraised the property at. Part of his logic was that, among other little extras, he had double nailed every stud for greater strength in earthquakes etc. I declined to take the listing on at his price and explained about the extras being of great comfort rather than great value. He was not impressed and he had a few words to say about my ancestry and honesty etc. Fourteen months later he sold the home for $11,000 less than I had appraised it for, as the market had since turned downwards. He met me in the street just after the sale and walked straight up to me. I was a little concerned at his approach but as he strode towards me he stuck his hand out and said, "It's sold and I don't want to talk about it, so shut up. Now, you were the only honest bastard that looked at my home so go find me a house for me to buy!"

I have to say, I love it when it happens that way. I did not sell his house for him but I was the only one with any credibility at the end of the day. Hang on a sec please; my halo is getting stuck among the keyboard.

Joking aside, my reputation was enhanced by turning down the listing and being upfront with my estimations of value. I told him what he needed to hear and not what he wanted to hear.

I just wish more salesperson would be brave enough to do that also!

Points to remember:
- *Your house is only worth what **someone else** wants to pay for it, Today !!*
- *Find out the level of your competition.*
- *Find out how long you may have to wait.*
- *Do something about it or sit back and wait.*
- *Don't blame the Salesperson if it doesn't sell on day one!*

Chapter 12 - Let's get down to negotiating!

This is the stage in house buying and selling where most dollars are won or lost. Pay attention and see how you would react to some of the scenarios.

Let's lock in two phrases that are well worth remembering when we are talking about negotiating

1. *A person's perception is that person's reality.* Say what? Perception is reality. If you believe that a property is great value then it becomes great value to you! The other party to the negotiation may not perceive the property as great value. To effect a sale, the Salesperson has to work on one party's perceptions.

2. *He who has the least desire has the strongest hand with the negotiations.* Put it simply, if one side is desperate to make the sale and the other side is ambivalent whether they sell or not, the one with the greatest desire will probably have to concede more ground on the price.

If we can take on board those two phrases we are more than halfway to understanding how to negotiate the best deal for ourselves and also how to influence our Salesperson to work stronger for us and make or save us a few dollars. Make that a few *thousand* dollars! I did promise that you could recoup the cost of this book possibly 100 fold and I meant it!

You like the home and you want to buy it. You have seen a dozen or more homes that compare and you feel that a fair price would be maybe $198,000 to $204,000. However, you figure you will try a low offer first and see how the vendors jump. The amateur Salesperson will spend the next twelve hours running back and forth between you and the vendor and each time the offer is moved $1,000 up by you and by $1,000 down by the vendor. You start at $190,000 he replies at $210,000 and after twelve hours of up and down alterations you meet in the middle with a messy looking agreement signed at $200,000.

Of all the 'jobs' in Real Estate, my favourite part of all of them was negotiating! To me it was, and still is, the most fun you can ever have with your clothes on! Don't get me wrong and assume I treated it lightly. It was also the most serious and. quite often, the most intense part of my job. Almost without fail, both parties start by adopting a posture that they won't pay more than…. Or they won't sell for less than… As you read through the next few pages, you may get an idea of how tough the negotiating can be. You may also get the sense of the sheer exhilaration of getting the two parties to agree on a price.

Many Salespeople will take the negotiating personally with the mindset that if they can't get an agreement together, they will not eat. My mindset was more focussed on how I could get the deal together and there were no negative thoughts allowed into that process.

Negotiating is like chess or checkers where you move human figures. I will warn you in advance that you may not like some of the tactics used, as the play is on all the emotions and senses. The bottom line is that the deal gets done with honesty and we have two satisfied clients, a buyer and a seller, and that is the targeted end result in any negotiation.

An aside here. You may remember that I have mentioned on a couple of occasions that there are (I believe) a great majority of Salespeople in the industry that are not 'too pushy' and will wait to be asked for the order to buy. Their reluctance to appear too pushy is down to a fear of rejection by their client in case their client sees them as a 'pushy Salesperson'. Rather than be rejected they will back off and try to appear as the nice guy. That fear of rejection also rears its head in the game of negotiating with negative results.

Nice guys never finish first in a sales or competitive environment!

What many Salespeople don't seem to realise is that they have been approached for their guidance in their role as a Salesperson. Being a nice guy / walkover is often frustrating to the client, when they want some leadership or guidance from the expert. What is more, they actually expect the Salesperson to be a little pushy and to try and make a sale.

The good Salespeople are not reluctant or scared to ask for the order. Their skill level is such that they can read simple body language, or other verbal and non verbal, gestures made by clients to know when is the right time to ask for the order or to back away from a 'close' as the property is not suitable.

My reason for saying the above is that the good Salesperson is usually the best negotiator as he welcomes pushing the boundaries that the lower performing Salesperson will shy away from because of fear of rejection. I will take it further and say that the good Salesperson should and will push the boundaries of each party's comfort zone to get the best price for either side. Often the negotiations can get tense and a little testy. The good Salesperson will hang in there. The poor Salesperson will back off in case they get rejected as the pushy one.

Often a Salesperson will receive instructions from his clients in negotiating that are firm and demanding in their bid to get a few dollars more (or less).

The buyer may say, "You can tell the vendor that I won't go a dollar over $196,000!"

The vendor may say, "I won't take penny less than $202,000!"

So what does the poor Salesperson in the middle say?

If he believed either party and relayed that instruction to the other side, their individual egos would probably not allow the deal to proceed further, which would then cancel out 50% of all negotiations that ever take place. The Salesperson should take on board the comments and then quietly ignore them. Treat them as posturing by both parties, who are trying to influence the Salesperson to work harder for their individual interests. You probably don't want to hear that do you? It happens, so deal with it!

A Salesperson's role is to negotiate between two parties, who each want to get the best deal for themselves. The Salesperson has a legal obligation to protect the interests of both parties. So, while you say you will offer the vendor $195,000 but you will go up to $200,000 tops, the Salesperson's obligations to you will not allow him to pass *all* of what you said on to the vendor. Likewise, if the vendor says he will counter-offer at $210,000 but will go as low as $203,000 the Salesperson would not be carrying out his duty of care if he passed on that information to the buyer. So the Salesperson is in a tricky situation that requires no small amount of skill and finesse. Each side will have a perception of the value of the property. I have already stated that their perception is their reality. Most times, the buyer's perception is lower than the vendor's perception.

One of the key things a Salesperson has to ascertain early on is:
Which side has the strongest desire to make the deal work?
Having ascertained that view, he realises that that is the party that will have to possibly make more movements in their offer or counter-offer.

For myself and with my negotiation experience, I would usually anticipate taking the offer to the vendor and getting their counter-offer back as the first opportunity to assess both parties desire to make the deal work. The second opportunity would be when I sat down with the purchaser to discuss the counter-offer. After I had met with both sides I had an idea of how the negotiating would need to be handled and which side would need to move furthest in their price. In probably six cases out of ten I could get full agreement without going into a third meeting as I always made an effort to get the buyer to put in an initial offer close to the stated maximum that they would pay. When I took that offer to the vendor I would ask them to give me the bottom line that they would accept. I would go back and tell the buyer that the vendor had said that "they feel that is as low as they can go". Using that phrase is a lot less confrontational than adopting a 'pay that much or forget it' approach. Most times the buyers would go with it or maybe try for another $1,000 off the price. Often they would ask me 'will they go lower?' As I stated before, this type of question puts the Salesperson in a very tricky situation legally. The usual reply here would be to the effect that, "I can't say what the other side's perception of value is in the home, but are you prepared to possibly lose the home for the sake of another $1000?"

Time for another little negotiating trick here, folks.

When I am negotiating, I am very professional and business like. I stress to both sides that we have an offer on the table that it should be considered seriously. The TV is turned off. We sit round the dining table and it is straight down to business. Seldom will it take more than ten minutes to arrive at a counter-offer figure, amend the contracts and be on my way back to the other party. I may only be gone from the first party for approximately thirty minutes and that includes travelling! How tough would you think the negotiating was if I arrived back at your door with a counter-offer in less than thirty minutes? To pad out the time, once I had the counter-offer signed, I might stop and have a chat and cup of tea with the vendors. I tell the vendors that it will make it seem I had a hard time working them down in their price. I would then arrive back at the buyer's home with the counter-offer after an hour and walk in saying, "Well, they did not take your offer so we had to do some negotiating, but I think you will be reasonably pleased with what they came back with."

Their perception is that I have been talking for an hour so it must have been a tough session. If the vendor became a little angry at the offer, I would not relay that information back to the other party. It's best to keep personalities out of the negotiating.

I do not disavow them of that perception that I have been talking to the vendors for nearly an hour. That perception is their reality and they look at the counter-offer with a little more validity. As I have said before, we want to get the best price that the buyer will pay for the property and that the vendor will accept. I am only doing my job, to the best of my ability, to be fair to both sides. The fact that the vendor and I sat and talked about the football for 30 minutes is irrelevant to the market value of the home, but the delay has given some weight to the counter-offer that we will now sit and discuss.

We have now reached the following stage.

The buyer was going to start at $190,000 and go to $200,000 tops. At my suggestion he opened with an offer of $197,500 and would only be prepared to negotiate to $200,000.

The vendor was going to counter at $209,000 and drop no lower than $203,000. He counter-offered at $205,000.
We are now sitting with the buyer and trying to bridge a gap of $7,500.

If we believe both parties and their initial statement *and* they go with their original limits ($200,000 and $203,000) we will have find a way to bridge a gap of $3,000 or the deal will not come together. This is where the fun starts as a negotiator. Getting the parties to come up to $200,000 and down to $203,000 is only taking the orders given to you and requires little or no skill by the Salesperson. This negotiation will usually take a little longer than the first meeting with the vendor.

How do we, as Salespeople, bridge the gap?

Firstly we don't try and bridge the gap. We state "The vendor is satisfied with all aspects of the offer other than the price, so that is good. It means that you can move in on the day you want and little Johnny can start school on the first day of term. The only thing he altered in the whole agreement was the price you offered. He has counter-offered with a selling price of $205,000. Does that sound reasonable to you?"

A couple of useful phrases

A couple of more tricks here folks there are two invaluable little phrases I taught my team to use.

"Does that sound reasonable to you?" If I asked you "will you pay $205,000?" your almost automatic response would be 'No'. By phrasing the question "Does $205,000 sound reasonable to you?" I am not asking you to pay $205,000. I am only asking you if it sounds a reasonable price. It is a totally different judgement I am asking you to make. It becomes a small decision (is it reasonable?) rather than the big decision (will you pay $205,000?). Remember earlier in the book when we talked about closing questions being small decisions rather than big ones. The small decisions bypass the need to make big decisions and it is the big decisions that make people frightened - of making decisions.

The other little phrase I use often is the phrase *"May I ask?"*

Preface a question with that little phrase and people answer the question as a continuance of answering the very polite phrase of 'may I ask the question'.

As an example, if I asked you how much you earned last year, you would probably tell me to get lost. If I asked the question 'May I ask, what did you earn last year?" you would probably answer "Yes, $37000, why?" I am not too sure why it works, but it definitely does!

For the double whammy of getting away with something that wants your co-operation the phrase I would use would be *"Does that sound reasonable, may I ask?"*

Getting back to the negotiation process.

Buyer- well it is a little more than I was prepared to pay
Salesperson – yes but would you be prepared to go up to $205,000?
Buyer. - Probably not, I would not pay any more than maybe $203,000 (the $200,000 has already gone out the door)
Salesperson- well. Would you be prepared to go to $204,000? (Remember, I am trying to get the best price for my Vendor!)
Buyer- no, $203,000 is my top dollar
Salesperson – well lets counter-offer at $203,000 and I will go back to see the vendor and see what I can do for you
If we had taken the initial statement of "$200,000 tops" the deal would have been dead and buried.

We now have to hope that the vendor remembers he only wanted $203,000.

In this book, it is a perfect world so the vendor accepted $203,000 and we have a deal.

That was simple and straightforward negotiation. If the Salesperson handles the parties well and with confidence, most deals can be handled as simply as this. As I said earlier, six out of ten deals can be done with only a couple of visits. If the initial offer of $190,000 had been accepted by the Salesperson, the vendor would have countered at $210,000 and the Salesperson would have been going between the parties for the next ten or twelve hours. The stronger or better Salesperson should be able to get the parties closer before the offer even goes on paper.

What if the offer is way below the vendor's expectations?

It is not a problem for the Salesperson. It only has to be handled in a different manner. It may be that the vendor is way over the top in his expectations. We would handle that in a different manner than if we perceived that the buyer was just trying to grab a bargain at $20,000 below value.

If the vendor was too high in his expectations. Say he wants $225,000 and FMV (fair market value) is $195,000 to $200,000. The offer comes in at

$198,000. We know the vendor will go ballistic when we bring the offer in so we have to be prepared for the meeting. When we get to the vendors home to discuss the offer. We only have one copy of the offer in our hands (the others are in the briefcase) We hold the offer in *our* hands and read out the details. Buyers name, settlement date, deposit, purchase price. At this point the vendor starts to blow. We then ask the vendor to hang on,' Let's go through the whole offer and look at *everything* in the offer, as there may be other parts we also want to change'. As we go through the offer we may repeat the price a couple of more times. Each time we repeat the price the vendor gets a little more used to the price and a little less insulted. It's a bit like when you stub your toe. The pain reduces quickly over the next few minutes unless you focus on it and then it gets worse.

After reading the offer through, we go back to the price and bring it forward for discussion. The vendor, usually, has now calmed down more than a little. At least he won't be thinking of shooting the messenger!

After listening to the vendor go on about how much his home is worth etc I bring the discussion back to the fact that we have a serious offer here that has to be considered.

Salesperson- "From what you are saying Mr Vendor you are not prepared to accept this price?

Vendor. **##2!!&+***(No)

Salesperson – "Well my role is to make the offer as attractive as possible to you. The offer is for $198000. If we could get the buyer to raise his offer to perhaps $202,000, would that be acceptable?"

Vendor - "No way I want at least $215,000" ($225,000 has already gone away from the memory banks).

Salesperson – "$215,000 seems a long way away from this buyer's offer of $198000. I cannot help but feel that we may scare this buyer away if we counter offer at $215000. Would you be prepared to sell for $210,000?"

Vendor- "Not a dollar less than $212,000 or it comes off the market!" ($215,000 has gone from the mind as well).

Salesperson – "So let's counter-offer at $212,000 and I will see what the buyer's response is."

The buyer is not happy. But he is surprised at the vendor dropping back to $212,000 after thinking the buyer's bottom line was $225,000

Salesperson – "Well, we have the counter-offer at $212,000. Does that seem reasonable to you?"

Buyer – "It is still way too dear. I can't see myself paying any more than $205,000."

The previous two examples are genuine cases that I dealt with. The second deal did not happen as the vendor held out for $212,000 and the buyer would not rise above $207,000. The point to remember here is the amount of movement that both parties made from their original starting mindset. I get tired of people who see Salespeople as always trying to push the sale through at any price. The above is an almost verbatim report of an actual negotiation. Don't blame the salesperson if one of the parties has an unrealistic expectation on price or value!

There are a number of points for you to consider from these two examples that may help to explain why a Salesperson does not always appear to listen to instructions.

- Just because a client states that he will not pay more than or sell for less than a stated amount is not a reason for the experienced Salesperson to accept that statement at face value. Possibly 40% of deals would be lost if we listened to a clients assertive statements which are often only stated as they believe it will make the salesperson work harder in their favour.

- Perception is reality. By delaying the negotiating process down, the other side believes we had a tough time negotiating with the first party and is inclined to give the counter offer a little more consideration.

- There is a psychology in delivering a low offer to a vendor. By only having one copy of the agreement on the table and by the salesperson holding that copy and reading it, the Salesperson can control, to some degree, the vehemence of the vendors over-reaction to the low offer. I call this technique the Butterfly technique. By mentioning the price and moving on, then touching on the price a couple of more times and moving on (like a butterfly), the Salesperson can judge when the vendor has calmed down sufficiently to be able to talk a little more calmly about the price and what we can do to make the price more acceptable.

- When the gap between the buyer's offer and the vendor's expectation is significant there is another wee trick to minimise its impact. If the gap is between a $198,000 offer and the vendor wants $218,000. We have $20,000 to bridge. If we keep mentioning the $20,000 or the $218,000 we keep reinforcing in the mind that we are talking of large dollar amounts and as we know, large dollars mean large decisions, which lead on to large indecisions. In this situation I would be using the tactic of saying 'how can we make this offer more acceptable? If we could get the buyer up to $203,000 would that be acceptable to you?' The mindset here is that we are making the buyer move up rather than making the vendor accept that he is, in fact, moving down. If we went the other way and asked the vendor to drop his price to $210,000, his mindset is automatically reinforcing, to him, that his ego wanted $218,000 and *he* is losing money. The walls come up and the deal becomes almost impossible to complete. This technique also moves the vendor away from a fixed position and makes him think more along the lines of what he *won't* accept rather than his previously fixed mindset of what he wants. The challenge for the Salesperson is to make the parties think laterally rather than stay with a fixed mindset.

- The time will come when there is a gap that cannot be bridged. The gap may be only $1,000 or it may be $10,000. At that point the Salesperson has to become the negotiator rather than the order taker. It is quite different skill and as I said earlier is the part of the job I get most enjoyment from.

- We have a legal obligation to present any (written) offer to a vendor. It is written into our contract of agency and is binding on us. I have heard instances where the Salesperson has declined to present an offer as the Salesperson thinks it is too low or a waste of time. No Salesperson on my team would remain on my team if he did that to a client. Ignoring the fact that we are breaking our contractual obligations to the vendor there is a strong possibility that we may be held liable for damages if the property sells for near that amount in the future. I am never concerned where an offer starts, as it is only where the offer finishes that is important. If a Salesperson declines to present an offer they are either lazy or lacking in confidence in their negotiating ability. Either way they should go and get some more negotiating practise or, better still, a different job!

The contractual obligation to present an offer actually can work in a Salesperson's favour. Occasionally we are told to present the offer on a 'take it or leave it' basis. 'If they don't accept it, tear it up' is also an instruction we receive. Daunting? Not really.

I'm going to digress for a moment and talk of a negotiating tactic I have used with success. When a vendor or buyer says something like,' I won't take less than..' or 'I won't pay any more than...' I have something of a quandary on my hands. They cannot back down without losing face. If I have to present a counter offer that is below the persons stipulated bottom line, I would only get one copy of the agreement out of my briefcase. I would tell them what the counter offer is and wait for them to blow up. I would confirm with them that the negotiations are at an end. Then I would slowly tear the single copy of the agreement in half.

Without fail, the party would look on in horror. Then they would realise their blustering has maybe lost them the sale. Then I would get the rest of the copies of the agreement out and invite them to tear them up, themselves. It brought everyone down to realising we are dealing with a live buyer/vendor and we should not let posturing get in the way of the deal. Manipulative? Maybe. Effective? Like you wouldn't believe!

Salespeople have an obligation to present the offers as stated earlier. The buyer gives the offer and the ultimatum. The Salesperson presents the offer to the vendor who counter-offers. As we stated earlier, once the offer is altered it is not binding on the offeree. When the offer is counter-offered, instead of the Salesperson holding an *offer to purchase from the buyers* we now hold an *offer to sell from the vendors* so he is obliged to present this offer back to the purchaser. Again, if Salespeople listened and followed every instruction from their clients, fully 50% of deals would never get done.

Are you thinking that all Salespeople are tricky and don't listen to instructions? In part, I would accept that as a criticism. In part, I would accept that as praise! Remember at all times, the buyer and sellers are the people who hold on to the pen and do the signing on the dotted line. The Salesperson's role, as the relative expert in the field, is to make sure that all avenues are explored in the client's wishes to buy or sell the home. Salespeople will explain the advantages and even cajole the clients along to encourage them to buy or sell, but at all times the client is the one who signs on the dotted line. If they did not want to, there is nothing that can be done about it.

Let's look at some negotiating lines

And while we are there, let's look at their counter arguments.

Remember the truism I gave earlier, the one about 'he who has the weakest desire has the strongest bargaining hand'? The following lines may be used against you as a buyer or a vendor to put the pressure back on you to make a compromise and demonstrate that you perhaps have the strongest desire (that means the least bargaining power!) to make the deal work.. The lines below are all intended to put the pressure back on the Salesperson or the other party to try and get the other side to move on their price. Be warned. By using these lines you may lose the buyer, **but** if you keep the buyer you should have made a few more dollars for your home. Good luck!

They can't afford to go higher than $198.000

- Well my home is on the market at $212,000, why did you bring them here in the first place?
- Why are they looking in a price range they can't afford? Were they hoping to grab a bargain?
- How did you qualify them as buyers for my home?
- Well they won't be moving into my place then, as they can't afford it.

They can't see the value in your asking price

- Well I can't see them moving into my home then.
- Are they professional valuers? Let the professionals put the value on the home after we have agreed on a price, my price!
- Can you tell me what other homes they are using to compare the values?
- So what, as the Salesperson, are you going to do to convince them of the value?
- As I recall, the asking price was set at your suggestion when you showed me the sales statistics for the area. Why not go back and show those statistics to them?
- You did tell them the asking price was only the asking price didn't you? I will negotiate

when they show me their real offer and not this insulting price that you have brought me.

- You have been telling me for 2 months that the public see my home as well priced. Why not use that same information and tell it to them.

We are only $5,000 apart, will you meet them in the middle

- If they give me an offer at the midway point, I will sign it but they will have to put their offer in to me first.
- Meet in the middle? Why should that be an indication of market value?
- No, I will drop $2,000 if they come up $3,000
- Aren't you supposed to be working for me? I will drop $1,000 and after that I lose interest in talking further.
- If they are only $5000 short of my price, I will drop $1,000 and they can have an extra two months for settlement to save the other $4,000
- I will leave the extra $5,000 in as vendor finance under a second mortgage for two years. How does that sound?

- I will drop $2,000 and take the dishwasher away when I move out if they come up $3,000.

They have been looking at a lot of properties and they are tossing up between yours and another one. If they can't get yours for their price they will put in an offer on the other home.

- Will you lose out on a commission if they do that? Yes? What are you going to do to convince them they should buy this one, then?
- Great. There must be someone out there who is sufficiently desperate to sell and will welcome their low offer. I am glad that I am not desperate to sell and can wait a little longer for the right person to come along that can appreciate the value we offer here.
- Let them go and look at the other home. You have been telling me for two months that my home is well priced and presented. There will be another buyer along shortly, won't there? However, if they do come back after trying the other home, I will probably be even more firm on my price. Please tell them that will you? Or they could save time by coming back to me with their best offer today and we will know if we can do business then.

The vendors won't drop below $209.000 (Put a fear of loss, of commission, in the salespersons mind)

- Well they obviously like their home, as they won't be moving out to let us move in. Please tell them that we won't offend them with further offers, as we are not prepared to go to their price.
- That is $12,000 above our offer; we won't be going that high, what other properties do you have to show us?
- Disappointing really as we would only go to $205,000. Pass our thoughts on to the vendor and we will look for something else tomorrow. (To partner) Did you cancel that appointment with Peter from (the opposition agency) ABC at 10.00 a.m.?
- Thank you for all your efforts with our offer. Maybe we should consider a different area, if we can't buy at our price.

The above (in Italics) are some of the most commonly used 'lines' that Salespeople use on a client to get them to move on their price. The required result is for you to make the next movement on your price. I have no problem with the use of these lines. I would have used something similar on a number of occasions with success. As you have read, there are a number of responses to those lines which are designed to put the pressure back on the Salesperson to go and have one more try on your behalf. Only use them if you have the nerve to give it one more go before you throw in another few thousand dollars on or off the price. They will work and work well. More importantly, if you have a Salesperson who is not at the top of the game, it will immediately peg you as the one with the least desire, so he knows he will have to work harder on the other side of the deal. Of course, if both sides of the deal are top negotiators or both have read this book you could end up with a standoff. Then the worst thing that can happen is the sale does not happen. Or we discover who *truly* has the least desire to make the deal happen!

A few general negotiating techniques that Salespeople use.

These are all further instances of the topics we have discussed earlier in the book.

When Salespeople get down to negotiating, they don't use the phrase "Two hundred and twelve thousand five hundred dollars". Firstly it is a real mouthful and secondly it is a figure that is larger than most people ever deal with in their day-to-day vocabulary. It requires a big decision which, as we know from earlier points, leads to big indecisions and a mild panic. It is so much easier to say"Two twelve and a half". Imagine how it sounds when the following situation arises. "They have declined your offer of two hundred and seven thousand dollars and have counter offered at their price of two hundred and twelve thousand five hundred dollars. If you will increase your offer by five thousand five hundred dollars we have a deal."

It took me the best part of a minute to even type that phrase. How much easier and comfortable is this "They wouldn't look at two oh seven and have come back at two twelve and a half. Will you come up the other five and a half to make the deal work?" The figures spoken have been simplified and the word "thousands" has not been mentioned.

Take it one step further.

♦ "I tried, but they are looking for another five and a half, does that seem reasonable to you?"

As we go further down the negotiating and we may only be $1,000 apart, we can reduce that even further.

♦ "For the sake of another one, you could lose this home, one thousand dollars is only an extra dollar a week on the mortgage. What are we talking about here? For the extra cost of, what, half a bottle of milk you could own your new home."

I used that approach with a young married couple that I had built up a great relationship with. The bottle of milk became "less than a packet of condoms a week! Go on the pill and you are ahead of the play and you have the home you want!" As I said, we had built up a great relationship, sufficient that I could use a jokey line like that. They bought the house but as for the condoms etc, our relationship was not that close.

Another little thing Salespeople use. If you are a buyer, they talk of the home. It is emotional with mental pictures of the warm fire and the smell of baking wafting from the kitchen etc. If you are a seller, it is called the house or the property. Figuratively speaking it becomes a pile of bricks and they try to take away the emotion from the negotiations. They try to present the home to the vendor as a commodity to be marketed, just like a can of baked beans and that is how it should be regarded!

Who makes the decisions? For the most part, Salespeople find that usually one person makes all or most of the decision to make the purchase. The other partner will contribute but as a general rule one person makes the decision to a greater or lesser extent. How do we discover who that is? There are some general guidelines.

Firstly, when you have the couple in the car and are taking them out to view homes, the one, usually the male, who sits in the front passenger seat of your car *usually,* makes most of the decision. It is a generalisation but it is usually pretty good.

On one occasion when we were buying a home for ourselves, the lady Salesperson really blew it! I wanted to sit in the back seat as I had a thigh injury that meant I had to spread out a little when I sat. My wife who had a quite senior position in local government took the front seat. At the time she out earned me while I was studying and she would own most of the buying decision as I got pretty fed up of looking at houses with my job.

The salesperson introduced herself and shook my hand and as an afterthought, said hi to my wife but did not shake her hand (first mistake). As we drove around her homes; she persisted in talking to me in the back seat rather than to my wife in the front seat (second mistake). I found the whole thing rather amusing as I was watching my wife's body language, which was very negative, and the Salesperson was not even noticing (third mistake). There was no way my wife could bring herself to even relax with this dummy, so there was no way we would be buying one of her properties. This lady was oblivious to the fact that my wife was going to be the decision maker, so was wasting her time. As I said earlier it is a generalisation about the front seat, but it is pretty good one to keep in the back of your mind.

Another way we pick out the decision makers is at the dining room table Not only does this tell us the probable decision maker, it also tells us the likely difficulty we will have with the negotiation. Concentrate please as we explain. Again, this is a generalisation but it works so many times it is something we watch for.

Most dining tables are the rectangular shape with one chair at either end and two chairs down either side. We always try to get the clients sat round the table. I always suggest that, as the contract needs to be read so we should use the table.

The Salesperson never sits down first, as he wants the clients to show their hand. The Salesperson only sits when the others are seated, so he can sit in a position where he can eyeball both people with minimum head movement.
The person who sits at the head of the table is *usually* the one who has most say in the decision. If the other partner sits close, they are in agreement about the decision needing to be made. The farther apart they sit, the less agreement there is on the decision to sell. Sometimes that salesperson is the referee between a couple splitting up. As I said earlier, the seating at the table is not a definite

indicator but it usually gives the salesperson a good idea of how tough the negotiations will be!

I seem to be presenting tips and tricks in no particular order. The fact is, there is no order to them. What we are offering to you is the variety of methods that negotiators use in the negotiating process. Sometimes they pull all of the tricks out of the bag sometimes only one of them. Some Salespeople have none of the skills in their armoury and that is why they do not succeed. The next little trick requires a lot of nerve **and** is best used by the best Salespeople. I have heard it called the 'lump of concrete' close. You will see why.

When the Salesperson has made his pitch, (be it for the listing or to get the client to move on their offer) he should speak to a point and put in the question and then shut up.

Completely.

Sit there like a lump of concrete.

Saying nothing

Until the client responds

The first one to speak loses!

I'll repeat that because it is important

The first one to speak loses!

If the client speaks it will generally be to move on his price.

If the Salesperson speaks it is to offer to soften the stance his previous request or statement made.

The first one to speak loses.

Half a minute of silence is a long time.
A minute seems like a lifetime.
The first one to speak loses

It is a powerful and effective technique to be used on the rare occasions when pressure needs to be put on a client to perform, or make a movement from, or even to reinforce, a previously held stance.
But....
There is a way of turning it around.
Turn it back on to the Salesperson by asking them a question...
Was there something else?
Is that your best shot?
You've gone awfully quiet. What happens next?

When the coach of a football or netball team is preparing for a big game, he wonders what tactics and strategy to use. Just suppose he was given a list of the strategy and game plans of the opposing team before the match. He would still have to make sure his team were well skilled in all the skills the game required and that those skills were practised to the stage where they became part of the players 'habit' level of competency. Then he could focus the players on overcoming the tactics the opposition would use.
In a Real Estate concept, the Salespeople have to practise and practise their skills until they can respond automatically to any given situation.

In America they have the annual conference of Realtors. Each year at the conference two of the top salespeople in all of the USA (both earn over the Million dollar mark!) have a standing agreement to meet in the bar before each NAR conference. Each place $1000 on the bar and try and close on each other with an imaginary deal. The best gets to keep the others $1000. The session can last for over an hour as most closes can be turned round with another close. The session usually attracts an audience of some of their contemporaries If it is good enough for those two, it is a good enough routine for me to emulate.

The best Salespeople who are already the best performers in those skills will constantly practise and practise to keep those skills high. Compare them if you will to someone like Christiano Ronaldo who, after training, would spend a further hour practising his kicking skills on his own. He was the best in the world at his position but to stay there he had to remain better than the best of the rest. His practising gave him a skill level that meant he could respond, *without thinking,* to any situation that arose during the game.

The top Real Estate Salespeople are like that. As in sport, there are various levels of play. Which type of player/ skill level would you prefer to have working for you to sell your home? An All Black or someone who cannot get a regular game with your local team's 5th grade side because they don't have the skill levels or they won't practise or train.

As I have said a number of times before, the commission you will be charged will be the same for the sometime 5th grade player or for the All Black player. So wouldn't it make sense to see if the All Black was available to work for you?

Points to remember
- *Negotiating is the most fun you can have with your clothes on.*
- *Whoever has the least desire has the strongest hand.*
- *Whoever speaks first loses.*
- *Does that sound reasonable?*
- *May I ask?*
- *Have an All Black as your Salesperson. You pay the same commission rate!*

Chapter 13 - FAQ. (Frequently asked questions)

Will you reduce your commission?

It happens occasionally enough to be a nuisance that the deal is only $1,000 apart and one of the parties asks a Salesperson to reduce the commission to make the deal work. Firstly I feel insulted. Let's say you worked at an engineering works. To finish an order off you stay behind and work until 11.00 at night. The next day, the boss says he won't be making enough money from that job so he won't pay you for the five hours extra effort you put in. How would you feel? Exactly! I may have been working for three or more months on this job of selling your home and to ask me to take a pay cut, now, is unreasonable. I have, on very rare occasions, dropped the commission on one deal if there were perhaps another deal or two depending on the outcome of this deal. Other than that I remember a former sales manager of mine responding to a similar request -

"Negotiate our fees? Certainly, we are charging you 4% of the sale price. I will gladly charge you 5% if you insist. Thanks very much."

Another way of looking at the problem is that, as the fees are based on the amount of the sale, every time the sale price goes down, the fees go down with it, so the Salesperson is reducing the fees proportionately. In a similar manner I would never reduce fees at the time of listing the property. The logic is that as the Salesperson works on a percentage of the gross commission, if they take a buyer to sell them the house down the road, they make X dollars. If they sell your house they make $500 less. Do you think you will get any action on your home from the rest of the sales team?

What happens at an auction? What about the phoney bidding I read about in the papers?

You can only see one bidder raising a hand yet the auctioneer is also getting bids from another party, but you cannot spot the other party. Um, that is because there may not be another party bidding. In virtually all auctions there is a clause that allows the vendor *or his agent* to bid. It is called 'vendor bidding'. The media have tried to make a big deal of the practise as auctions have become more popular and the newspapers have a 'slow' news day.

The current Auctioneers Act has been in force since 1917 and the concept of vendor bidding has been enshrined in law since then. Here is the rationale behind it. *Provided the auction is subject to a reserve price and that a reserve price has been set,* the vendor bid is a declaration by the vendor that he will not accept a bid any lower than his own last bid.

The reserve price is the minimum price at which the vendor will authorise the auctioneer to sell the property unless there are other bids that will take the price higher than the reserve price the vendor has set. Work with the following typical scenario.
You, as a bidder, bid $190,000 (and the rises are in $5,000 lots).
The vendor bid comes in at $195,000 and the auctioneer calls out for a bid of $200,000.
You bid $200,000.
And the vendor bid comes in at $205,000.
You can be sure that the reserve is set higher than $205,000 or the vendor would back away from the bidding.
Eventually the bidding reaches $214,000 and you are the successful bidder. That means the reserve may have been set at $212,000 or $214,000 and you have reached or exceeded that reserve price.

Often the auctioneer will be calling the bids on behalf of the vendor. It is called 'pulling bids' and the auctioneer will pull these 'imaginary' bids from a colleague in the audience who will not make any gestures whatsoever, or he may pull them from the lamp stand with the comment. "Looking for $205,000 and we have $205,000 at the back thank you. (Now looking at you) Sir, will you work with me for another $5,000. $215,000 to stay in the hunt" etc. If you have difficulty accepting the arrangement of vendor bidding, don't buy at Auctions! Be aware that nearly every type of auction I have ever attended as an auctioneer, or as a prospective buyer, has used the vendor bidding. So don't be fooled by the media into thinking it is only related to real estate transactions.

In actuality there is very little difference here than you would get if you were negotiating under the normal routine, where your offer to buy is declined and the vendor counter-offers. Often a buyer will not enter the bidding until the bidding gets somewhere near the price he is prepared to pay. This is one of the reasons the auctioneer gets the ball rolling with the vendor bidding, to see who is out there looking to bid.

Auctions are exciting if the auctioneer is competent and controls the crowd well. In Melbourne, nearly 80% of all properties are marketed with an auction programme.

Another thought for you to go away and think about is that in Australia, USA, Great Britain and New the sales statistics are very similar. Around 60% of properties sell pre-auction, 10% sell 'under the hammer' and 20 % sell post-auction.

What is a Market review meeting?

The listing Salesperson should hold a meeting with his vendor every two or three weeks to discuss the progress on the marketing of his home.

Ever heard the saying *"If nothing changes, then nothing changes!"*

If you are on the market and have not yet sold, despite the Salesperson's best efforts, something has to change.

You have several options in how to change or energise your properties profile.

- Reduce or remove the price
- Change the marketing style
- Increase the profile
- Remove the home from the market.

Your Salesperson should be looking to get your approval to change something in your marketing strategy at every marketing review meeting - If nothing changes, nothing changes!

Reduce or remove the price. Remove the price completely and advertise the property as "Offers" or "POA". You should attract buyers that are from outside the buyer range you have been targeting. Possibly you may get an offer that is 20% outside your price expectations but you will have to live with that. At least you are getting some interest. Another word here. If your home is priced at, say

$200,000 or more, a price reduction of $2,000 or $3,000 will have no effect at all. The reduction has to be in the region of $10,000 to have sufficient impact to make a difference. A significant price drop will allow the salesperson to revisit past clients through your home with the 'Good news'.

Change the marketing style. If you have been working as an exclusive agency with a set price advertised, consider advertising with a price band. Even more advantageous to you, would be to consider undertaking an Auction programme, which leads me onto the next point.

Increase your profile. Can you say, with all sincerity, that McDonalds burgers are the tastiest in the world (sorry about that, Ronald McDonald). It is only a personal opinion, but I don't think they are even close to being as filling or as tasty as you will get from the local café. So why do McDonalds sell so many million burgers worldwide every second of the day? Right, it is because of all their advertising, isn't it! Are you with me on this? Take it a step further. In the Major Herald every Saturday there are approx 25,552 (on average) homes advertised. Ever heard the following expressions.

You only have 15 seconds to make a good first impression.
You never get a second chance to make a first impression

Look at the first saying first.

In the newspaper you don't get fifteen seconds for that first impression. You have approximately just one second or even less to make that first impression, as the viewer's eye skims over all those 25,552 homes that are your competition. The viewer only looks at the headline and moves on if the headline does not grab him. The whole elimination process can be over in less than a second and your chance to make that first impression is gone.

Fortunately in newspaper advertising you do get a second chance to make a first impression. If you have a large advert in next week's major daily newspaper etc, the reader will not remember last week's 3-line profile among the plethora of all the other adverts. So make this week's advert bigger, to stand out from the crowd. The bigger advert will not guarantee a sale but it does raise your profile so, even if your home is mediocre in appeal, at least it will be noticed. And, hey, it works for McDonalds. Invest some 'significant' dollars into your marketing.

Take it off the market. This is often the most overlooked option taken by both vendors and Salespeople. Take a reality check at the review meeting. Be specific to the Salesperson. Tell him you cannot or will not sell for less than X dollars.

What are the chances of you getting that amount? If the Salesperson is on top of his game, he should be able to tell you your chances of achieving your aim. If the answer is that you stand no chance while the market is down, why put yourself through the mental anguish of being in the market at all? Be realistic and remember that no amount of advertising is likely to get you another $20,000 more than your home is worth when compared honestly to its competition, unless you manage to snare an uninformed buyer which is a 1000-1 shot. You may have a better chance of winning Lotto than selling your home at $20,000 over its FMV.

Save your time and effort and take it off the market, until the market rises to meet your expectations. The Salesperson may fight you on this, as, without listings being advertised, his name will not appear in the newspaper etc. Be realistic. If all the overpriced homes were taken off the market, the supply / demand ratio would improve dramatically, the market would become more positive and, who knows, prices may rise to get closer to your expectations.

Sources of buyer feedback

- Open home viewers

- Kerb crawlers

- Other Salespeople on the team

- The listing Salesperson

There are 2 types of Salesperson feedback to be aware of.
- Feedback
- No feedback.

Let's look at the second type first.

The phrase 'deafening silence' springs to mind. You are aware of the people who come to the open home and give you feedback. What about all the people who don't come to your home? The people, who see the sign on the lawn, pull up, take a look from the road and then drive off. The ones who pull up to the open home, but don't get out of the car and drive away again. In politics, they call it voting with your feet! You don't like what you see, or you perceive it as not good value and you stop further interest and go look at the next home. Take a good look at your home from across the street and see what it tells you about how the place appeals to a first time viewer.
- Gutters dirty and overgrown.
- Lawns need mowing
- Trees need trimming
- Front windows need painting.
- Gardens need weeding.

Your front view says an awful lot about you and your home to someone standing on the street. That is why the big chain stores such as Macy's spend so much time and effort on their shop windows. If the display looks good it will entice the buyers in. A shop window that is dirty, has dust on the products, dead flies on the floor will tell a customer a lot about the store. They shop with their feet and don't enter the store. It is the same with your home. The garden and the front face of the home are your shop window. How can you spruce it up to promise even better things inside?

That is the 'No feedback' side covered. Now let's look at the sources of actual feedback you receive

Weekly written reports.
These should have a summary of all the people through and their comments. All comments should be recorded, good or bad! Use these weekly reports as the foundation of your market review meetings.

A phone call from the Salesperson when they have taken a client through the home.
As they bring a client to your home, each salesperson should each leave a business card so you know that someone has been through. One Real Estate group introduced a system where they had the marketing folder left at the home in a prominent position. Before a Salesperson, with a client, left the home they were expected to ask the client their

thoughts and fill those comments in inside the listing folder.

Weekly inspection sheets.
Back at the office, a good number of agencies have what is commonly called a weekly inquiry sheet. The sheet has columns for enquiries, which may be split into sign, advert or phone inquiries. Another column for inspections, one for open home visitors and a last column for comments. Each Salesperson is expected to enter all enquiries they have received for each individual property during the last seven days. It only takes five minutes to complete. The list is prepared in price order. The benefit of this list is that the vendor gets feedback and comments from all the team rather than just their own Salesperson. The side benefit is that it is very easy to spot if one or more price ranges are more active over a period.

The Salesperson should be giving you as much information as he can gather about your property and its competition. So that you can continue to make informed decisions about your home. Be wary if your weekly reports are all positive or even just neutral. If your home is not selling, you should be receiving the bad news that it is perhaps too dear or there is a major flaw that all the buyers have spotted. Without good feedback you cannot make good decisions.

How do I know if I've got a good Salesperson?

Be aware that you have a whole team of Salespeople working for you. and not just your listing Salesperson. All the other Salespeople back at the office are also contracted to promote the sale of your home. How good are they? There is a simple way to find out, ring them up. If you are a little nervous, get a friend to ring them for you.

Pick out the ad for your home or an advert for a home that you know is quite similar and ring each Salesperson at home. Ask a question about the home that is not covered in the advert (does it have a large lounge?) and see how they respond.

There is a technique to hold a caller and turn the caller into a client that any numbers of good Salespeople use and it is quite effective. Briefly it involves taking control of the conversation and is quite simple. We have covered the technique in an earlier chapter and it is well worth trying when you are looking to take on a salesperson to market your home. Alternatively, use the technique when you want to know what the salesperson is saying about your home. Phone the Salesperson up about a similar property to yours that can be dismissed easily. Then ask about the other home they have listed at (your address), can you tell me about that one? You may be delighted with their response or you may be horrified. At least you know what they are saying and can do something about it.

Do I have to have Open homes?

It isn't compulsory, but they are strongly recommended. Most buyers today spend their time going through Open Homes and that is where the Salesperson meets them for the first time. As an estimate, probably 70% of first contacts are made through the open homes. Unfortunately, not all Open home viewers are serious buyers.

On average, the people who call into view an open home fall into three categories.

One third are looking to buy. We don't really know which are the buyers until we talk to them. Then we have to know which category buyer they are, A,B or C.

Remember, we talked about A,B and C buyers in an earlier chapter.

One third are looking to sell. Possibly, they are here to compare prices or even to see how the Salesperson operates as he may be on their shortlist of Salespeople they want to work for them in the marketing of their home

One third are wasting time or being nosey. They may indicate they are selling or buying but the Salesperson still needs to qualify them correctly. All open home viewers are accorded respect, even neighbours or friends of the vendor. But buyers do tend to receive more attention. After all that's what the Salesperson is there for, isn't it?

Is it worth advertising my home on the Internet?

Is it good, bad, or brilliant?

I have positive views about the internet. From an Agency point of view, it is another expense that the offices have to fund that can easily cost up to $4,000 or $5.000 a year or more. That extra cost is usually not recoverable. Because the other offices have it, we have to have it or the public perception is that we are not working with the latest technology. Most buyers, today, are computer savvy. Most of the homes on the websites have interior pictures. That already makes the internet browsing better than driving around the neighbourhood. Unfortunately, like the newspaper with so many adverts, it can become an eliminating process rather than selection process.

Is it cost Effective? It's hard to say, there are a number of cases where we are told of the sale being made to an overseas buyer who never set foot in New . I personally doubt that the commission gained from the total number of sales made from the Internet is even half the amount that Real Estate Offices spend on the Internet. The Internet approaches are only replacing what used to be done by mail a few years ago. The value of the Internet is the immediacy of information. Don't misread me please. I am a devotee of surfing the internet in my spare time and spend a good number of hours per week researching on the Internet. I just have doubts that the Real Estate hype of having your home listed on the Internet is of as much value to you as the Salesperson would make out..

Do you remember back in the 70's when there was only one TV channel to advertise on. That channel had a market monopoly in all age groups. It was easy to make your advertising decision and which medium to use. Now there are so many channels plus another hundred odd on Sky TV. The net effect is that we do have to advertise where the competition is advertising. So the decision on where to advertise is harder and it also ends up costing more to get that broader coverage.

And who pays for all this extra advertising? Obviously it falls back on you as the end user because the Offices have to charge you higher prices to cover the higher costs. Ever looked at it from that viewpoint?

What is the difference between buying at auction and the more usual Sale and Purchase agreement?

We have already covered the sequence of buying in these two styles. What I will comment on here is the difference in safeguards that the buyer has.

In the more usual method of buying, there are a number of safeguards written into the small print that protect the buyer's interest. The main ones being that the buyer (or more usually his solicitor) has 15 working days to requisition the title. That means that the buyer can call for a certificate of title and check that there are no defects on the title. A Title search can reveal such things as the house is being sold by the registered owner, who owns any mortgages etc, check on caveats or restrictions or easements or right of ways etc. If there any defects that show up, the deal may be cancelled or amended. The vendor also gives a number of guarantees that are tucked away in the small print. The key thing here is that the buyer has 15 days to check things out after the deal has been signed.

With the sale at auction, the buyer's guarantees are quite restricted or, in some cases disappear completely. The contract for the sale is quite different and the small print also does not offer many of the guarantees. Before the auction takes place, the terms and conditions of the Auction are made available to all interested parties. Any person bidding on the property is deemed to have made themselves familiar with the property and is buying after examining all the properties records that are available and, having assessed that information, is deemed to be bidding on their own judgment of what the property is worth. So the guarantees are gone!

If you analyse the process, when you buy under the more usual method, the buyer makes an initial *offer to purchase* and lays out all the conditions under which he will make that purchase (settlement date, subject to finance, which chattels are to remain etc) if the vendor accepts that offer in all its parts, then a deal is made.

In auction, the situation is reversed. The vendor is standing up (or his agent, the auctioneer) and *offering to sell* the property under the terms that *he* selects (settlement date, must be a cash deal, which chattels he will leave with the property, reserve price etc.) and is stating to the world at large that these are his terms of sale, is there anyone who would care to make him an offer, He will sell to the person who makes the highest offer (bid) if the reserve price is met or bettered. If you are intending to bid at Auction, always do your homework on the property first and <u>always</u> check the terms and conditions before bidding

What is a Mortgagee Auction?

First let's establish what a mortgage is exactly. A mortgage is not a loan! That may come as a surprise. The loan which you commonly call a mortgage is correctly called....a loan! The banks however want some security for their money that they lend you. Your promise to pay is not sufficient for their needs. So you let them have your home as a security for the loan. The security you give is called a *mortgage.* The term mortgage comes from the two French words mort (meaning death) and gage (meaning agreement). So the word mortgage literally means an agreement until death. Now let's look at the semantics of it. Remember if you will that the person who donates blood is called a 'donor'. The person who receives the blood is called a 'donee'. The giver ends in "or" and the other party ends in "ee".

With the mortgage, you as the borrower give to the bank a mortgage on your home so you are the *'mortgagor'* and the bank who receive the mortgage become the *'mortgagee'*. So when you hear of a mortgagee sale it is because the banks are exercising their power as the *mortgagee.* Usually because the mortgagor has defaulted on the payments of the bank loan and the security is being sold off in order for the bank to get its money back.

An anomaly when purchasing by mortgagee auction is that the chattels are not included in the sale. The reason for this is that the bank will not take the value of the chattels into their calculations when determining how much security they require. Chattels, as we know, are things like carpets, curtains, cookers, light fittings etc. These are portable and easily removed and are not considered to be secure enough to be termed as security. Logically then, when a bank sells up the property to recover its money it cannot claim security on, or sell, the chattels as they were not offered as security. The next step of course is that the owner (mortgagor) can take the chattels away when they move out. So after all the above, be aware that when you buy a mortgagee property you may not get the chattels.

Another curly thing for you to be aware of with mortgagee sales is that the mortgagee does not, and cannot, guarantee you vacant possession. If the mortgagor elects to stay put, the cost of getting them evicted is all down to you. Both situations mentioned above happen very rarely, but you do need to be fully aware of them when you bid.

Thinking of buying the property as a rental investment?

It's a good idea provided you make the decision to buy according to the market and its demands.

Fifty years ago New had one of the highest rates of home ownership in the world with something like 91% of people owning their own home.
By 1992, that 91% had dropped to 81% private ownership. Put that down to perhaps the shutting down of the Housing Corp and its cheap loans. There has been talk within the last few years that the level of private owner occupation could be as low as 60% within the next 10 years.

Fortunately, or unfortunately, the Government had put fear into Kiwis by stating that there would be little or no retirement pension available in twenty years time (or words to that effect) and people had seen the purchase of rental investments as a good long-term investment. By using the equity in a home, you could purchase a rental property for no money down and the tenants would pay off the mortgage so when you retired in fifteen years time you could sell off the rental home and have a lump sum of maybe $200,000 to retire on.

I have wondered on more than one occasion whether the closing down of the Housing Corp. and the statement about the pensions were somehow related in an effort to make Kiwis buy up the old state houses. That would however require some forethought and planning from the governments. I am digressing, do forgive me.

Back to the 'rentals' thing. There have been experts popping into print over the last few years forecasting that by 2020 we may be down to only 50% of privately owned and occupied homes. As this is becoming something of a trend worldwide, there may be some validity in their assertions. Later, we will talk on house leasing. It is a relatively new and fascinating concept.

What has this trend done to our buying demographics? For one thing, it has kept the Real Estate industry afloat for most of the last five years. Is that a bit of an eye opener for you?
Think of this, possibly twenty percent of all homes sold in the last five years have been to rental investors. As in all new trends in, when we hear of the latest way to get, save or make money we, as a nation, tend to jump onto the bandwagon with a passion. Within two or three or four years there is an oversupply. People then try and jump off the bandwagon. Usually all at the same time and prices fall like a stone due to there being an excess of supply over demand. Who is going to buy in, when prices are dropping?

Eventually the market settles down when the nervous nellies have got out and prices start becoming steady and profitable. If you don't believe me, think of trends like kiwifruit, deer, angora goats, fitches, walnut trees, llamas, and the list goes on. Take deer, for example. At the beginning, stags were fetching $20,000 and more. After 18 months they were down to around $700. Today, there are a number of operators making very good money out of deer. The ones who get in *and stay* are the ones who make the best dollars.

Rental properties have gone through the same phases. Everybody jumped on the bandwagon, prices went up, an oversupply of stock became the norm so the rentals charged to tenants had to be reduced to get and retain tenants. Lower rental incomes meant lower returns so rental homes went back onto the market resulting in an oversupply; prices dropped through the floor.

The situation today is that we have an oversupply in some price ranges, which reflects in the rentals being charged. Other price ranges are fine and demand is high. The supply / demand factor will vary from area to area. My advice before buying is to find a well-recommended property manager and ask their advice on what price range to buy in. Invite them to view the home before you buy and assess the likely rental the home will attract. This will assist you in your finance calculations. I have always used a property manager to manage my rental properties as I cannot stand having to chase tenants for overdue rent etc and property managers are specialists in rental and tenancy law.

Earlier in this segment I asked the question, in relation to a falling price for rental properties, who will buy in at this point? If I were genuinely asking the question, the answer would probably be along the lines of – the smart investors looking for a long term steady investment. Rental properties will always be in demand in most areas. If you look at rentals as a long term buy you should be on a good steady earner if you buy wisely.

I've heard about House leasing. What is it?

Although it has not yet taken off in many countries, the concept of leasing homes is attracting interest in other countries and is well established in America. To differentiate between a tenancy and a lease is not that easy, but in a general concept it is a little easier to explain. We associate the word lease with the leasing of commercial space and offices etc for, say, a term of three or more years with rights of renewal and a wordy lease document. Tenancies, we equate to a residential home with the tenant only giving three weeks' notice to quit etc and a simple tenancy agreement to sign. Even though we hear of some tenants staying for a number of years, the average tenancy would be for an average of four to nine months. The tenant has little security of tenancy if the owner wants to move in or sell the property and can be kicked out with as little as 6 weeks' notice.

Having a lease agreement for a three-year term or even longer is satisfying the housing needs of a number of overseas people who want security of tenure. The lease agreement is quite wordy and may detail such things as who pays the rates and repairs. How often the landlord should redecorate the home etc.

With inflation being fairly low and consistent, there is a growing feeling that the money you would normally tie up in your home may be put to better use over a five year term. That money when invested may get a higher return than if you sink it into a home. Even though you still have to pay rent or lease. That rent cost may be offset by the mortgage you would not be paying. A client of mine paid $210,000 for a townhouse four years ago. When he approached me to seek advice I looked at his whole economic set up. He and his wife had an income of $67,000. They had been paying off the mortgage (sorry, I mean Bank loan) for four years. The loan outstanding was now down to $152,000 (from $172,000 four years ago) and the house was valued at only $186,000.

I rearranged his loan structure so that his 21-year mortgage should be paid off in eleven years and recommended that he invest $20,000 of his savings into an investment that should return him around 9% per annum. If he leaves the $20,000 invested to compound for five years he should be able to pay a significant amount off his mortgage and have it paid off within a further three years. If he had actually leased a home on day one with his $50,000 deposit he would be sitting at least another $140,000 to $200,000 better off in eight years time over and above his residual home value and he would not have been liable for all the repairs and rates on the unit he had bought.

I know that this arrangement depends on the person having a deposit for a home and also that there are investment avenues open to them that pay an amount in excess of inflation plus rent. But when you balance the mortgage payments you make on a home against the use of the money tied up, it does not take long to be on the winning side if you allow the investment to compound.

When to talk to your solicitor.

Whenever you want to speak to him, feel free to speak to him. Most Real Estate offices have an excellent working relationship with the local solicitors. They have to! The solicitors can ruin a deal quicker than any other party. Conversely, the income derived from conveyancing would be the bread and butter income of most law firms. Both Real Estate Offices and Lawyers have to work together and, for the most part, the relationship is mutually supportive and beneficial.

Be aware that some solicitors charge for everything they say to you and if you are not careful, you can quickly run up your bill. For a simple thing like conveyancing, a legal assistant does the bulk of the work, as it is a fairly easy and mundane task. My reason for saying this is that if your solicitor is the best and dearest in town, you may be paying 50% more for the conveyancing of your home than you need to. In our town the costs for conveyancing for the vendor can range from $600 to $1350. Mind you, when you go to the dearer office you do get a nice cup of tea with a chocolate biscuit. Most Salespeople can recommend a solicitor that specialise in conveyancing at a reasonable cost, unless you particularly like chocolate biscuits.

For other matters such as questions on parts of the agreement, the Salesperson should be able to explain them quite competently. However,

if you have any doubts or concerns re the legal side of the agreement, please talk to your solicitor. He/she is the person most capable of explaining the legalese and settling your doubts. Talk to the solicitor before you sign the agreement if you have a doubt!

Can I cancel my Agency contract (Listing Authority?)

Yes and no is the best answer I can give! Within reason, you should be able to cancel your contract of agency at any time. However as you have a binding legal agreement with another party (the Agent) the cancellation is at the discretion of the Agent, if he is prepared to accept the agreement between you being cancelled. It has happened on a number of occasions that the Vendor has been approached by a third party to do a private deal and 'do the agent' out of his fees. It doesn't happen often but it does leave a nasty taste in the mouth. Agents generally are very obliging when a Vendor wants to take the home off the market, but you should always remember that the Agent and the Salesperson have already invested a significant amount of time and finance on your property.

If you are withdrawing from the market, the Agent may release you from the agency agreement on the understanding that if you sell during the unexpired term of the agency or sell at any time to a person that was introduced during the term of the agency, you will be held liable for the agency fees.

If you want to cancel this agency agreement and move to another agency, then the Agent is quite entitled to refuse to release you unless you can prove that the Agent has done something significantly in breach of his undertakings to you. This happens very rarely and is usually the result of an underhand Salesperson from the other company coming in the back door and making promises to the vendor about what they can do for the vendor. Usually, only an underhanded vendor will listen to an underhanded Salesperson. To my mind they were always well suited. I would usually release them and then wait for the new agency to try and introduce one of our clients so we had a wee argument inter-agency. The industry authorities don't like clients to be involved in inter-agency disputes as to who gets the commission. So they minimise the risk of clients paying two lots of commission. However always be aware that you may be open for paying two lots of fees when you chop and change agencies.

What if I want to complain about the Salesperson or the Agent

Whatever your complaint, you should direct the complaint in the first instance to the Agent or licensee of the Salesperson concerned. The Agent should try to address and satisfy your concern as the next step involves the Agent, him/herself, being hauled up for a disciplinary hearing if you take it to the next step.

If you can't get satisfaction from the Agent, your next step is to write a letter to the local regional office of the Real Estate authority. Your letter will be acknowledged and several things happen. You will receive a letter back telling you that the Authority will take the matter further if you want them to. Be aware, however, they cannot make the Agent or his Salesperson make any restitution to you if that is your aim.

The Authority will investigate your claim and, if the complaint warrants the step of disciplining the Agent or Salesperson, they will take that step on your behalf. It can be a long process but the Authority is ever mindful of its public image and does take all complaints about it's members very seriously.

My house is so special I deserve a better price than my neighbours.

Life is not always fair. You are probably best advised to market your home with an auction programme and see what is the best offer that a buyer will pay for it Always bear in mind that 'special' homes are often limited in their appeal to a wide range of buyers. We need to get at least two people interested to get that premium price for you. Are there two people out there that agree your home is special?

I have been with one company for 3 months and they have not sold it. Should I change agency?

What have the Salespeople been saying to you during the marketing? If they have been giving you advice that you have been ignoring, there is little any Salesperson can do for you. My experience has been, almost without exception, that if company 'A' cannot get you your price of $230,000, then company 'B' will fare no better. Provided you are satisfied that company 'A' has done a good job of marketing your home there is usually very little extra that company 'B' can do for you. How does the Salesperson feel about your home? Is he still enthusiastic? Probably the only reason that I would change Salesperson is if I felt that the Salesperson had lost interest or enthusiasm.

After six months with the same company I would be seriously considering whether I had to be on the market rather than deciding between companies.

Do I list with a big company or a small company?

That's a tough call. Usually the smaller offices are more proactive for their smaller client list. On the other hand, although your listing may get lost among all the other listings that a large firm will have, the larger firm will usually have a significantly higher number of buyers to show your home to. On the laws of probability, I would go with the larger firm. However, having said that my prime concern would be working with a Salesperson that had been recommended to me. If none of the Salespeople that had been recommended to me worked for the largest firm in town I would not be using the larger firm.

What is this 'referral network' that I keep hearing about

Working with a brand name does have a number of advantages to a vendor. If I single out the 'Century 21' group it is because I have just received their flyer in my mailbox. They have some 8000 offices in 27 countries. The referral network comes from each of the offices being obliged to pass on the name of anyone they hear of who may be moving . That is what I call a pretty impressive referral network!

What are my options in arranging finance?

Most people still go along to the bank and ask for a 'mortgage' (bank loan). The bank will give them the loan provided the applicants can offer sufficient security and demonstrate that they can comfortably repay the loan over the term.

Do you really know what options are available to you?

Most people are not aware, as they only arrange this type of loan every seven to ten years so they rely on the experts.

Like everything else in the world, banking has changed and there new options available to you that could save you money. Lots of money!

One of the first things to consider is, whom do you go to for the loan?

Increasingly we as Real Estate Salespeople are recommending that buyers use a mortgage broker in preference to going directly to a bank. There are a number of reasons but let's only look at two or three of them.

- Firstly, many of the brokers offer us a small commission for introducing the client. It may only be $50 or $100 but it is an inducement. Some of the banks are now also offering an introduction fee, but we will still, as a personal preference, be recommending the brokers for the following reasons.

- Secondly, each bank has a different lending criteria. Some may stipulate that a borrower can only use up to, say, 35% of their income for servicing their total debts. When you include car hire purchase and credit card repayments that sometimes does not leave much for the mortgage payments. Other banks may have a policy that you need $200 per week for a couple to live on plus $50 for each child. After that amount is deducted the balance may be used for debt servicing. By going to the bank first, you may have to wait four or five days to be told that you don't fit their lending criteria and your application for finance is declined. Often there is now insufficient tine for you to approach a second lender before the agreement's deadline for arranging the finance is past.

♦ When you go to a broker, the broker will examine your personal circumstances and make the approach to the bank whose lending criteria is most appropriate to your own circumstances. The brokers work almost exclusively on commission so they do tend to work harder for you to get the loan if you are a marginal case.

♦ Another excellent reason why I recommend mortgage brokers is that, for the most part, banks will charge you a loan fee of between half and one percent of the loan amount which can often reach $1,000 or more. The brokers will often get this fee discounted or even cancelled depending on the bank and the broker. We were in the ludicrous situation in 1992 where we wanted to be loyal to our bank, who had stood by us through a fairly lean time. When I rang my personal banker to enquire about a loan he told me there would be a loan fee of $850 to pay. On the advice of a colleague I approached a broker we were recommending through our office. He arranged the loan quite capably with no loan fee. The loan was arranged at my own bank! What made it even weirder, is that the bank then paid a commission to the broker for introducing our loan application! If they had not requested a loan fee, I would have dealt direct. As it was, they lost a further $600 in the commission to the broker. There has to be some logic in there somewhere but it eludes me! P.S I also got the usual $50 fee from the broker for the business!

♦ The final reason for considering a broker is that by approaching a bank directly they can only sell you the products that they have available. The broker may have access to all the banks plus they may have access to non-banking sources of finance that offer a better interest rate for low risk level borrowers. Insurance or finance companies are often on their contact list. Non-traditional lenders often do things differently and often to the benefit of the client. My own home loan is through a Dunedin based company who are consistently a quarter of a percent lower in their rates than the banks. This company only has one office to service all of New so they can keep their costs down which is a benefit to me in the rate I pay.

Fixed or floating rate?

It is always a judgement call on this topic. Ideally you should have some in both types. For myself I have a floating rate revolving credit loan (more on that later) with part of that loan separated on a 1 year fixed rate. The floating rate at the time was 8.5% and the fixed rate was 8.1%. On my mortgage of $150,000 I fixed $50,000 at 8.1% and left the balance on the floating rate, my logic was that as the bulk of the loan was servicing my rental property investments I wanted to be able to sell the rentals and reduce the loan without the penalty of breaking a fixed term loan. Within a month of me fixing the rate on part of the loan at 8,1%, the interest rates reduced and my floating rate is now down to 7.00%. You win some and you lose some. As I said earlier, it is a judgement call and only time will tell you if you made the right decision.

Types of loan

Interest only. Usually, the banks will only allow you to have an interest only loan for a period of three to five years. Back in the early 1980's, inflation meant that after three years your $100,000 home had increased to perhaps $140,000. You took out an interest only loan and then sold it after three years to make a profit. Nowadays, inflation is under control and interest only loans should be considered mainly where you could guarantee some increase in income during the 3-year period so that you can manage the payments when you have to revert to principal and interest payments or some other form of windfall that will reduce the principal significantly.

Principal and interest repayment. Over a predetermined term of perhaps fifteen to twenty five years. Payments remain constant if the interest rates remain static. Each payment consists partly of paying the interest and the balance goes to wards reducing the principal outstanding. This is probably the preferred or usual loan arrangement for perhaps 90% of all home loans. Initially the monthly payment is 99% interest and 1% principal repayment. As time progresses the interest portion decreases until by the last year of the loan the interest may only be accounting for 5% of the monthly payment. The principal reduces quite slowly with this type of payment. As an example, assume a $100,000 loan taken out over 25 years. The monthly payments are within a few cents of

$1000 per month. After 6 years, the borrower has repaid to the bank ($1000 times 12 months times 6 years) $72,000. The rub here is that of that $72000 only $6000 has gone off the debt and the interest paid amounts to the not insignificant amount of *$66,000.*

Table mortgage this type of mortgage is quite uncommon in New . Basically the borrower pays off a set amount of principal every month *plus* the interest for that month. In month one you may pay $300 off the principal and (say) $925 in interest making your monthly payment $1,225 in month one. In month two the interest is slightly less so your payment is reduced to perhaps $1,221 and as the loan progresses the monthly repayments reduce until in the last month of your loan the monthly payment may only be $311. Although the initial monthly payments are higher the nett effect is that you pay a significantly lower amount of interest over the full term of the loan.

Revolving credit line. You should treat this like a large overdraft and realise that the less you owe to the bank each month, the less interest you will have to pay monthly. The key factor for this account to work for you is to have all your income going into the account and only spend the money when you have to. The longer you keep the money in, the less interest you have to pay out. Assume you have a nett income of $40,000 and your outgoings are

$20,000. The balance of your income, $20,000, should remain in the account to keep your outstanding amount to a minimum. What usually happens with the other types of mortgage is that we pay the bills and pay the mortgage and the rest manages to slip through our fingers. Each year perhaps $5,000 can slip through your fingers. If you monitor that $5000 it could be going to reduce your balance in the home loan account and the savings can be quite significant. One good example of this type of loan. A young couple had twenty one years left to pay on their mortgage and owed $158,000. Their combined income was $71,000. By converting to the revolving credit line they will have their loan paid off in just under eleven years and will save between $100,000 and $121,000 in interest payments.

Chapter 14 - Final Thoughts.

It is just an observation on my part but Real Estate marketing is reflecting ordinary marketing trends. There are a number of products coming onto the market with a fanfare that are not necessarily new products but more in the way of old products that are being finetuned, repackaged and marketed with a fear factor. Often there is no tangible benefit to the end user. Other companies, in an effort to keep or boost their market share, have to come out with a copy product or develop an alternate fear factor. Let me give you some everyday examples in the milk, soap powder and painkiller product range.

Milk used to be milk! Pure and simple, straight from the cow as Mother Nature intended. Now we can only get treated milk. In possibly seven different types such as low fat, high calcium, hi energy, sterilised, goat's milk. Mother's milk. The latest type is milk specifically for Children. Scientists would have us believe that the new milk is better for us. But which one? Did you really know that Mother Nature's milk was doing you that much harm when you were growing up? Are we losing the plot here or are we just falling in to some marketing ploys built on a fear factor?

Washing powder. I do concede that the days of rubbing your clothes on a stone, down by the riverbank,, needed some attention from the marketing department. We developed washing machines. Then we developed Automatic washing machines. Can our laundry get any easier? Our soap powder had to go through the development as well. It went from washing machine powder to Automatic machine powder to cold-water powder. Then we developed fabric softener in two or three varieties. The latest 'fear factor' marketing is a new product that disinfects the clothes and cuts down on the transmission of body fungi that are 'transmitted' in the wash process. Did you know that your life was being harmed by the antics of your clothes in the washing machine before the scientists and marketing people told you about it? Do you really believe them? So what is next? His and her washing machines that are built to be gentler on her more delicate clothes etc?

Painkillers. I find it hard to take this one. One of the painkiller manufacturers is, at the time of writing, running a large ad campaign that tells you they now put a cellophane wrapper around the outside of the packet to give you 3 way protection. It doesn't improve the product at all. It increases packaging costs which you, the end user will end up paying for. The other manufacturers will have to copy the packaging to keep up which has a nett result that all 'over the counter' painkillers will go up in price for the same *unimproved* product. Somewhere along the line the end user, that's you and me, loses out!

My reason for stating the above is that there is a parallel to the Real Estate industry. What worked well 10 years ago still works today. But we as an industry are building into our product ranges all of the extra's (Auctions, Internet presence, Colour advertising etc) that do not necessarily provide a better or different product to our end-users. For the most part the new services or products we introduce give us a short-term edge over our competition. Once our competitors copy us, the advantage is gone. However, we often are committed to keeping that product in our product range and also into our cost structure. As I stated earlier, the prime example of this was the introduction of colour advertising in the newspaper. One Company in our town started to advertise in colour, so eventually all the Offices were using colour in their adverts. What started out as a distinct advantage to the first company has been minimised once everyone is using the colour adverts. The nett result is that every office now has to find an extra $18.000 every year to pay for the extra cost of colour in the advertising!. That $18,000 is the equivalent of an extra 7 sales per year to be completed. OR the vendors will have to cough up with some major extra advertising dollars. The nett result is that you the clients have a largely unimproved product and it is costing you more dollars. I have ideas on how to stop this happening but it will involve every office in a location to sit down and agree to stop (for instance) using colour adverts. The big winners are the newspapers and other media who benefit by an increased turnover. The losers are the end users. That means you guys, our clients, who are at the end of the billing chain.

In our defence I will say that this is not only in regard to real estate, it is in every product we buy. Maybe it is time for a customer revolt. That is not going to be covered in this publication. If you will remember very early in this book I stated that our industry deserves our fees because of the somewhat speculative nature of our business. I hope that by now you have a better idea of how our industry works. I also hope you are better prepared to handle the stresses of buying and selling your home. At least you are better informed!

I hope you have enjoyed the contents of this book.. I hope you have also learned of a few of the tactics that the Industry will be using to make the sale. If you know the tactics you can plan accordingly. By being aware of some of the negotiating tactics we, as an industry use, you should be able to save a few dollars on your purchase or be able to resist the temptation of dropping your price too quickly, when you receive an offer to sell.

There are Salespeople out there who are great at working with buyers but not so hot at working with vendors. Indeed there are Salespeople who were used to buy a home but the client would not have them near when they come to sell the same home, as they do not want to be subjected by the Salesperson to the same amount of pressure from the buyer.

In closing I give a salute to all the Salespeople and agents who are doing a great job, giving great service and getting a good reward for their 14/7 week. They are giving great service and treating the Real Estate industry as a worthwhile career. As a reader of this book, your role is to make sure you get one of the good guys to market your home or help you to complete your next purchase. I hope this book and its contents have been of help to you!

I wish you the best of good fortune when it comes to buying or selling your next home.

Points to remember:
There are far too many. Maybe
you should read the book again.
Take notes this time.

---

www.ingramcontent.com/pod-product-compliance
Lightning Source LLC
Chambersburg PA
CBHW071415180526
45170CB00001B/107